ORIGINAL MUSIC FOR MEN'S VOICES A SELECTED BIBLIOGRAPHY 2d EDITION

By WILLIAM TORTOLANO

The Scarecrow Press, Inc.
Metuchen, N.J., & London
1981

Library of Congress Cataloging in Publication Data

Tortolano, William.
  Original music for men's voices.

    1. Choral music--Bibliography. I. Title.
ML128.V7T66 1981   016.7841'063   80-25917
ISBN 0-8108-1386-6

ACKNOWLEDGMENTS

Grateful appreciation is extended to several friends and colleagues who very kindly researched titles, read many pages of the manuscript, and allowed me to reprint from their publications.

The Intercollegiate Musical Council sent me all issues of their journal, Quodlibet, and gave permission to use the article by Marshall Bartholomew, "The Intercollegiate Musical Council, A Bit of History."

Robert Johnson's excellent article "Learning a Song by the Barbershop Method" is very happily included. Mr. Johnson also provided information about SPEBSQSA (The Society for the Preservation and Encouragement of Barber Shop Quartet Singing in America).

Dr. James Fudge's extensive research on the Male Choral Music of Franz Liszt is included with much appreciation, as is a section from the fine doctoral dissertation of Dr. John Lundberg, "Twentieth Century Protestant Male Choral Music." To both gentlemen, many thanks.

CONTENTS

Part I

Part II

INTRODUCTION TO THE SECOND EDITION

In its second edition, Original Music for Men's Voices: A Selected Bibliography has almost doubled in size. In addition to new music that has been published and several titles that were overlooked, the enlarged catalog of compositions includes many that are available through foreign importation. Also, many works have been found in the collected edition of a composer.

This second edition includes several articles by recognized choral experts that relate to music for male voices. Kindly reprinted with permission, these are: an article on the method of learning a barbershop song, by Robert Johnson, Director of Musical Education and Services of the SPEBSQSA, Inc.; an interesting account of the early choral activities of the Intercollegiate Musical Council, by Marshall Bartholomew, the distinguished late conductor of the Yale Glee Club; sections on the early glee clubs in England, taken from John Lundberg's doctoral dissertation, Twentieth Century Male Choral Music Suitable for Protestant Worship; an extensive article on the music of Franz Liszt, by James Fudge; and excerpts from the doctoral dissertation The Mass and the Twentieth Century Composer (settings by Krenek, Harris, Harrison, and Langlais), by William Tortolano.

Other features new to this edition are a bibliography pertaining to both original music for male voices and related studies, and a listing of service and professional music organizations of interest to male singers.

The publishing trade is often in a state of flux, with one company buying another. To take account of this, the

1

list of publishers and their addresses and telephone numbers
has been brought up to date.

The index of authors and translators reflects the increased size of the listing of musical works in the catalog.
Dates of authors and translators have been included when possible.   The catalog entry is given after each name.

Extensive cross-references have been added to the
index of titles.   These include the original language when not
English, and the translation.   Often first lines are also provided, if they are not the same as the title.   The catalog entry is given after each title.

Also reprinted in this edition is an article by Robert
Grose on Title IX, legislation passed by Congress in 1975,
which has had a profound effect upon the male (equal-voice)
choral group.   Many colleges and schools felt that the legislation prohibited one-sex groups as being discriminatory, and
consequently dropped these groups.   Other institutions had become coeducational during the late 1960s and into the 1970s.
It seemed unnecessary for some to maintain two equal-voiced
choral groups (male and female).   Instead, they created or
amalgamated into mixed-voice groups.

It was a period of chaos, and unfortunately many outstanding male choral groups were disbanded.   But a careful
reading of the original document does make it clear that
it is in fact possible to continue an all-male, or all-female
choral group.

PART I

BACKGROUND: MUSIC FOR MEN'S VOICES

"For many years it has been common to hear conductors of men's and women's choruses complain about the lack
of a central bibliographical source to which they might turn
for good material." So states J. Merrill Knapp in his Selected List of Music for Men's Voices, published in 1952 by
Princeton University Press. Now out of print, Merrill's List
suffers from the persistent problem inherent in any such study:
new material is being published and old titles are being with-
drawn. Nevertheless, Knapp's book has a wealth of information.

The task of finding original music for men's voices is
often frustrating. There is much music of quality, but unlike
the availability of music for mixed voices, one must constantly
seek out titles, composers, and publishers from a maze of
information for the enterprising choral conductor. This is
disseminated in a variety of publishers' catalogs, foreign and
domestic; the collected works of composers; and many other
sources. Considerable time, therefore, can be spent in seek-
ing quality music. To seek the significant, the distinctive,
and the aesthetic from the many titles available is always a
challenge.

In addition to Professor Knapp's serviceable book, one
can find useful lists in the publications of the American Choral
Foundation. Also, Professor Kenneth Roberts of Williams
College has written A Checklist of Twentieth Century Choral
Music for Male Voices. His titles are often fascinating, including little-known works by Scandinavian composers. The
unavailability of a large portion of these works does not make
the checklist any less valuable as musicological research.

5

The problem of finding quality music also applies to
music for women's voices. Although there is a considerable
body of composers and appealing texts for both women's and
men's voices alone, one must look harder for it, as the pre-
dominant part of the world's greatest choral literature is
largely for mixed voices. In the category of music for wom-
en's voices, A Selected List of Choruses for Women's Voices,
by Arthur Locke and Charles Fassett (third revised edition,
1964, Smith College), is estimable. Also helpful is Charles
Burnsworth's Choral Music for Women's Voices (Scarecrow
Press, 1968). Both books, and other studies, can give clues
to possible material for men by the use of the term "equal
voices." Some compositions lend themselves to both voicings.

A serious problem confronts the compiler of any such
list. What should be included? A maze of entangling questions unfolds. The first problem is to indicate those works
that are specifically written by the composer for adult male
voices. A second problem is to limit criteria to those compositions that are not arrangements, folk or otherwise. Boy
sopranos, castrati, male altos, and countertenors present
special problems. But, if one starts the search with the
premise of adult male voices, a large, exciting list can be
developed.

A great source for male voices is German Männerchor
music written during the Romantic era. A large number of
scores poured from German music presses to satisfy the need
for music for this popular community and parlor art. The
pens of Mendelssohn, Brahms, Reger, Cornelius, and, in
particular, Schubert and Schumann, were especially prolific.
Not all is of equal quality. Yet, for the sake of completeness,
this study has included available examples from the era. The
curious can find unusual texts and instrumentation. Practically all are eminently singable.

Understandably, some of these works are of secondary
merit, but are historically of interest as well as revealing
of the facets of a composer's style. Even the "greats" would
often write simple, performable music of secondary artistry
in order to make a living or conform to prevailing standards
of the day.

Regretfully, much interesting material from Scandinavia
is usually omitted. Some of it, by such composers as Sibelius, is of real merit. However, a good segment is untrans-
lated, and the language difficulties could be extensive. Al-

though many pieces are out of print, or not normally available, they are listed whenever possible. American composers
of the Romantic era who received their training in Germany
also wrote music in this style. Many such pieces are by
MacDowell, Chadwick, Foote, and Horatio Parker.

Because many conductors are affiliated with liturgical
churches, this study includes textual sources of practically all
works so listed. This makes their seasonal or liturgical pro-
priety clear and functional. Besides, one can assemble programs of particular textual preferences. "Anonymous" is here
used for those texts that are quite well known but have lost
specific author-identity in history. In particular, one finds
this the case with medieval liturgical texts of the Roman
Catholic Church and Hebrew liturgy. The Roman Breviary
and the Liber Usualis, often the source of many texts, seldom
specify an author. Instead, a general reference is given, such
as "Medieval Text." Texts in honor of Mary are often difficult to identify. "Unknown" refers to the lack of information
of any source whatsoever.

The Bible (particularly the Psalms) is the most popular
source of textual inspiration. Until quite recently, there has
been a variation in numbering of the psalms for Catholic and
Protestant Bibles. The latter is the usual numeration (King
James) followed in this study. When the Biblical title is
given by the composer in Latin, an English translation is usually provided. The same is true of non-Biblical sources.
Some French titles almost defy translation, such as the Poulenc works. Debussy's "Invocation" is a superb work, little
known, by the great master of Impressionism. Schubert and
other German Romanticists are, in most cases, listed in the
original and in English translation--especially famous works
like Schubert's "Widerspruch," or Contradiction.

Certain composers, like Bach, are available in several
editions. In such cases, a generally accepted, musicologically
correct version is listed together with one or two other possibilities. In the case of Bach's Cantatas, the Breitkopf und
Härtel editions and the Henry Drinker editions are listed. An
excellent source of information about the Cantatas is Werner
Neumann's Johann Sebastian Bach's Handbook of Cantatas,
published in German by Breitkopf und Härtel.

Although "arrangements" of folk music are largely excluded, it was felt that composers of the stature of Holst,
Vaughan Williams, Bartók, Grieg, Stravinsky, Kodály, Pou-

lenc, Copland, Moussorgsky, and Harris should be included.
In these expressions, they went beyond ordinary arrangements in the commercial sense and add an inherent style,
personality, and contribution.   Bartók's use of folk melody,
for example, is not merely literal repetition of a tune, but
a significant impregnation of the composer's style.   In a
sense, the original melody is almost recomposed through
harmony and other techniques.

        It could be a detailed study in itself to analyze the
"correct" spellings of different composers' names.   One
recalls immediately Vittoria versus Victoria; Handl or Gal-
lus.   It was decided to use the spelling that seemed preva-
lent among most publishers.   In this case, it would be Vittoria and Handl (not to be confused with Handel).

        The updating of not only the Catholic Church but
many other Christian and Judaic denominations has replaced
many traditional texts.   All of the Latin Masses included
(and there are many first-rate ones, including those by Harris, Krenek, Langlais, and Villa Lobos) utilize the traditional Catholic text.   A new English Mass text appears in 1969,
but so far few major talents have set it to music.   The almost mandatory inclusion of a congregational part has so
far not been of significant importance to the great composers.

        The area of Mass settings for all voices (from 1903,
when the Motu Proprio was written, to 1964, when the Second Vatican Council promulgated its Constitution on the Liturgy) is analyzed in detail in William Tortolano's doctoral
dissertation: The Mass and the Twentieth Century Composer, University Microfilms, Ann Arbor, Michigan.   The
largely undiscovered Psalms by Benedetto Marcello (fifty
of them), not all for men's voices, offer, in English translation, a great potential for the liturgy.   These works are
in a variety of vocal and instrumental combinations, all
quite functional for new liturgical innovations, vernacularism
and practicality.

        The Broadway theater, however expressive of the
American scene, must of necessity be largely excluded.
First, many octavos are pure arrangements; and secondly,
few are of high artistic quality.   Their popularity bears little relevance to valid inclusion alongside the works of Beethoven or Wagner.   But there are some exceptions, such as
"The Fugue for Tinhorns" from Guys and Dolls or the almost completely male musical, 1776.   Student songs from

colleges have been essentially recomposed by men like Orff and Johann Schein. They have, therefore, been included in this study.

The opera, in particular works by Verdi and Wagner, offers a truly marvelous storehouse of first-rate original male music. One can also find examples by Weber, Beethoven, Mozart, Rossini, and others. Often, it is possible to delete a part, or parts, for women's voices, as it is common to find equal-voice doublings. One such example is the "Chorus of Hunters" from Rossini's William Tell. The elimination of soprano and alto causes no noticeable loss. The general unavailability of Russian operas, including those by Glinka and Prokofiev, somewhat limits what is an exciting repertoire.

Specific ethnic connotations offer exciting repertoire enrichment. Folksong arrangements often clearly reflect a people's experiences of lifestyle. Bartók and Kodály are great masters. Jewish composers are increasingly developing a modal style that offers innovative challenges. Earlier Jewish composers, such as Salomone Rossi and Lewandowski, are not easily identifiable ethnically, except through the use of Hebrew texts. For further help, one should consult the helpful collection Cantorial Anthology, by Gershon Ephros.

Although not originally intended for male chorus, the Bach Cantatas contain rich possibilities. Many of the tenor-bass duets (soloists) are conducive to many voices. The availability in English translations and the editorial work of Henry S. Drinker make them recommendable. They are of course not part of a Männerchor tradition, but are worth looking into, nevertheless.

Some composers issue the same works for both mixed and equal voices. Copland's opera The Tender Land and Gretchaninoff's Russian anthems are such examples. Mostly, music for mixed voices (though arranged for male voices) is not included. The exceptions are those composers who specifically approve of arrangements or do their own versions (e.g., Gretchaninoff). In a few cases, where the composition is so famous that it almost defies exclusion (e.g., Arcadelt's "Ave Maria"), it was felt that reference should be made.

A common complaint of conductors who direct choirs

of limited vocal resources is that there is a lack of "easy"
unison or part music of quality: "Gebrauchmusik," as Hindemith called it.   Suggested composers to research are Hindemith, Altenburg, and Lou Harrison, among many.   Harrison's "Mass for Male and Female Voices," for trumpet,
harp, and strings (also called the St. Anthony Mass), is
based on authentic Indian melodies from Spanish Colonial
California.   It is a gem.   It is possible to perform it with
men only, but perhaps it loses much of its "color" and effect thereby.   Yet, it is included because of its unusual texture and unique melodic genesis.

        The availability of good music for choirs of limited
resources has always been a serious problem.   Most of the
great composers have not written simple music for such
groups.   It is possible, nevertheless, to discover in history
some exceptions, although not necessarily for equal voices.
Schubert's "German Mass in F Major" and the hymns of
Louis Bourgeois are only two such examples.   World Library Publications has issued an extensive series of motets
for small Catholic choirs to be used on various Sundays and
holidays of the liturgical year.   Although not all are excep-
tional, one can, through careful selection, find several interesting works; in particular, those by Richard Felciano
and Leo Sowerby.   Concordia Publishing House has produced
a similar series for Lutheranism.   It is important to add
that their intention was not strictly to be denominational.
Instead, one can discern an ecumenical flowering.   Also of
worth is the series Cantor-Congregational Responsorial, from
GIA Publications.

        Canada has a diverse heritage: English and French.
In addition, it has encouraged ethnic immigration since
World War II.   Both English and French schools are well
established.   Canadian composers of music for men's voices
are represented by the high artistic standard of Jean Pa-
pineau-Couture, Healey Willan, and Claude Champagne.

        Black music, other than spirituals (of which there are
an enormous number of arrangements), is almost devoid of
works for men's voices.   The black composers Fela Sowana
of Nigeria and Ulysses Kay of the United States are exceptions, but their works do not show any ethnic influences.
Poet Langston Hughes is used by Anthony Donato in his
"Homesick Blues," as is Paul Laurence Dunbar in Henry
Cowell's "Day, Evening, Night, Morning."

        The generally growing acceptance of serialism and

electronic music is vastly neglected in choral literature.
Future potential is evident in Richard Felciano's Pentecost
sequence with electronic sounds. The Schönberg pieces are,
of course, acknowledged serial masterpieces. Ernst Křenek's
"Missa Duodecim Tonorum" is a unique setting of the Mass
for equal voices.

Some works have provocative titles or stories. One
such example is Philip James's "General William Booth En-
ters Heaven." Booth was founder of the Salvation Army,
and this setting is highly evocative of the Army's spiritual
heritage and atmosphere. An enigmatic work is Roy Harris's "Mass for Male Voices and Organ." Rarely sung and
now almost a curiosity item, it deserves hearing. The composer found himself at odds with ecclesiastical authorities at
Saint Patrick's Cathedral, by whom he was commissioned
to write the work. In a New York Times interview, he
said that composers put a price tag on music. The church
authorities were highly offended, and the event seems to
have been unfortunately misunderstood. One of the most
challenging works is Martinů's "Field Mass." Written as
a memorial to Czech dead in World War II, it is scored for
a large wind ensemble and voices. The instrumentation,
however, is not available in piano reduction.

When a choral extract is taken from a large work
and is not available as an octavo, the piano-vocal score is
listed as primary source. Often, the entire choral parts
are available. "L'Enfance du Christ," by Berlioz, contains
one particularly effective section for men's voices with bass
solo. Although the men's chorus is not published separately,
the entire choral parts are available.

In regard to practicality, those works that involve a
large orchestra are here listed also in piano reductions if
so available. "Rinaldo," by Brahms, would probably be
performed more often with piano accompaniment than full
symphonic instrumentation by most men's groups. However,
the instrumentation is listed. It would be relatively easy
to obtain it from the publisher. Stravinsky's "Oedipus Rex"
demands a fairly large ensemble with specific instrumentation that is an integral part of the work. The piece is rarely if ever done with piano alone.

One serious problem is to determine just what is
"original" for men's voices. One recognizes that vocal
timbre has changed, and that boys and men singing soprano
and alto were intended in former practice. Although boys

are still an integral part of Continental choirs, they are
less common in the United States. Rather than eliminate
all the music that was written with this voice disposition
and, therefore, eliminate a rich literature from contemporary use, it was felt best to include this music (mainly Renaissance, and English of the sixteenth and seventeenth centuries) in editions of equal voices for men. The Italian Casimiri was particularly successful in editions of Renaissance
polyphony adapted in this combination.

Knapp says, "Some composers, when they used the
term 'ad aequales,' also expressly designated that the composition could be sung by either high or low voices as long
as they were equal. This meant by men an octave lower,
if the original notation was for high voices, or by women
an octave higher if the original was for low voices. While
this was apt to be true of the seventeenth century, it is by
no means always true of the sixteenth, and it is well known
that music which sounds well for women's voices often becomes muddy and thick when transposed 'down' an octave
for men." One successful example that is adaptable to both
scorings is Villa Lobos's "Mass in Honor of Saint Sebastian."

An attempt is made in this study to provide as complete as possible a listing of music available from commercial publishers in the United States or from European repre-
sentatives. These are accessible for purchase or in some
cases rental. For help in locating some interesting material in this category, the reader is referred to the catalogs
of American Composers Alliance or Composers' Autograph
Publications.

Besides titles, composers and their dates are included, together with scoring for voices, soloists, accompaniment, instruments, language, text source, publishers, catalog numbers, and other pertinent information. Collections,
such as Schubert's music, are included, as they are fairly
accessible in libraries and other central depositories or have
been issued in inexpensive booklet form.

First lines have been included when they differ from
the title. If only the title is given, the first line is the
same. Unless a foreign title is known exclusively in that
language (e.g., "Ave Maria"), an English translation has
been included. When the author or source of the text is
known, this information is included.

Except for music of great merit, tradition, and
fame, art- and solo-song arrangements have been excluded.
For practical reasons, few examples before circa 1500 are
included. This is one of the hazards of bibliographical veracity. One must draw a line somewhere.

The reader is referred to the recent publications of
reproductions in small score of the complete music of a
composer. All of Schubert's music for male voices is now
available in four small-score booklets at an inexpensive
cost from Edwin Kalmus.

Russian liturgical tradition offers beautiful selections,
largely for male chorus. Unfortunately, not much is available; but the persevering conductor can often find material
by writing or visiting Orthodox Churches. England has produced a quantity of high-quality glees and choral music for
equal voices. Although this music has the advantage of being in English, its suitability to equal-voice choruses is com-
plicated by the fact that the English, particularly in cathedral choirs, use almost exclusively boys for soprano. The
alto is sung by a male (countertenor), or, less rarely, boy
altos. When women sing this part, they are designated con-
traltos. Although some are not pure adult male-voice compositions, this listing does include several male-voice editions based on boy soprano and male alto parts.

This presents a difficult problem for those countries
where only adult males sing the parts. Unfortunately, this
precludes use of much music in the United States by male
choruses, including works by Byrd, Purcell, and other English masters. When editions are published that are designed for all adult male voices, these are included if they
are practical and incorporate musicological veracity. When
known, ATBB adapted for TTBB has been indicated.

Many Renaissance motets are designated as being
for "equal voices": ad aequales or cum paribus vocibus.
When clef signs are clear, one encounters little difficulty
in identifying such as soprano, soprano-alto, alto, tenor,
tenor-bass, and bass. These generally indicate some combinations of high or low voices. One can also investigate
the range. Some writers claim that "chiavete" implies
transposition. The basis for inclusion has also been to
some extent the actual sound in performance and whether
it is clearly articulated. If a "muddy" sound results and
lines are foggy, then this can be considered a reason for

not including the piece.   The clef does not indicate the
voice part, per se.

        Useful references on texts and helpful interpretive
guidelines to choral music, especially Bach Cantata, can
be found in Henry Drinker's catalogs of the Drinker Choral
Library.   In addition, his Index and Concordance to the English Texts of the Complete Choral Works of Bach, Bach
Chorale Texts with English Translations, and Melodic Index
and Texts of the Choral Works of Bach in English Translation are valuable.

        No claim can be made herein to absolute comprehen-
siveness.   The question of whether a piece is an arrangement or not has at times been difficult to determine.   Oc-
casionally, exceptions are made.   One such is "Simple
Gifts," arranged by Irving Fine and used in Copland's bal-
let "Appalachian Spring," itself based upon a Shaker melody.

        In Biblical references, Arabic numerals designate
chapters or psalms (except where a composer specifically
does not do this) and verses.   Whenever possible, timings
of compositions are given.   This information was generally
drawn from three sources: the duration of the music as
given by the composer or publisher (not a usual practice);
recordings; actual performances.   Although duration may
understandably vary from performance to performance, an
attempt has been made to give some practical help, whenever possible.

        The raison d'être of this volume is to present in one
place as complete a list as possible of music for men's
voices, with helpful references of stable value.   It should
aid directors in expanding their repertoires, thereby saving
many hours of frustrating research and fostering some challenging programs.

ABBREVIATIONS OF TERMS

A.	alto
acc.	accompaniment
adap.	adapted
ad lib.	ad libitum (at pleasure)
anon.	anonymous
arr.	arranged
attr.	attributed
B.	bass
Bar.	baritone
bn.	bassoon
br.	brass
BVM	Blessed Virgin Mary
ca.	circa (about)
Cent.	century
cl.	clarinet
Col.	Colossians
comp.	compiled
cont.	continuo (figured bass)
Dan.	Daniel
div.	divisi (divided)
dbl. cor.	double chorus
ea.	each
ed.	edited by, editor, edition
E. hn.	English horn
Eng.	English
ev.	equal voices
fl.	flute
Fr.	French
Ger.	German
H.	high
harm.	harmonized

Heb.	Hebrew
hn.	French horn
hndbl.	handbells
HSD	Henry S. Drinker
Hung.	Hungarian
It.	Italian
L.	low
Lam.	Lamentations
Lat.	Latin
Matt.	Matthew
mix cor	mixed chorus
mvt.	movement
Norw.	Norwegian
ob.	oboe
oct.	octavo
op.	opus
opt.	optional
orch.	orchestra
org.	organ
perc.	percussion
pf.	pianoforte
Phil.	Philippians
picc.	piccolo
Port.	Portugese
pts.	parts
pv.	piano-vocal score
Ps.	Psalm
rec.	recorder
S.	soprano
Sp.	Spanish
stb.	string bass
str.	strings
T.	tenor
timp.	timpani
trans.	translated
tromb.	trombone
unac.	unaccompanied (a cappella)
unis.	unison
va.	viola
vc.	violoncello
vers.	version
vln.	violin
vol.	volume
vs.	verse, verses
wds	woodwinds

Numbers after orchestra (orch:) refer to the
instruments, e.g. , 3232/4231/timp/str, means 3

flutes, 2 oboes, 3 clarinets, 2 bassoons/4 French
horns, 2 trumpets, 3 trombones, 1 tuba/timpani/
strings.

PUBLISHERS' ABBREVIATIONS AND ADDRESSES

AAC   Association of American Choruses, Drinker Choral Library, c/o The Free Library, Logan Square, Philadelphia, PA 19103.

AB   Annie Bank, c/o WL

ABIN   Abingdon Press, 201 Eighth Ave., Nashville, TN 37202. (615) 749-6459.

ACA   American Composers Alliance, 170 West 74th St., New York, NY 10023. (212) 362-8900.

ALB   Alexander Broude, Inc., 225 West 57th St., New York, NY 10019. (212) 586-1674.

AMP   Associated Music Publishers, 866 Third Ave., New York, NY 10022. (212) 935-4240.

AR   A-R Editions, Inc., 22 North Henry St., Madison, WI 53703. (608) 251-2114.

ARIS   Arista Music Co., Box 1596, Brooklyn, NY 11201.

ARR   Arrow Music Press, c/o BH

AUG   Augsburg Publishing House, 426 South Fifth St., Minneapolis, MN 55416. (612) 332-4561.

BAR   Barenreiter Verlag, c/o EAM

BB   Bote and Bock, Berlin, c/o AMP

BELMONT   Belmont Music Publishers, P.O. Box 49961,
              Los Angeles, CA 90049. (213) 427-2557.

BEL   Belwin-Mills Publishing Corp., 26 Deshon Dr.,
              Melville, NY. 11746. (516) 293-3400.

BH   Boosey and Hawkes Inc., 30 West 57th St., New
              York, NY 10019. (212) 757-3332.

BHL   Breitkopf und Härtel, Leipzig, c/o ALB

BHW   Breitkopf und Härtel, Wiesbaden, c/o AMP

BIRCH   Birchard and Co., c/o SUM

BLOCH   Bloch Publishing Co., 915 Broadway, New York,
              NY 10010.

BMC   Boston Music Company, 116 Boylston St., Bos-
              ton MA 02116. (617) 426-5100.

BMI-C   BMI Canada, Ltd., 41 Valleybrook Dr., Don
              Mills, Ontario, Canada. Also c/o AMP

BOU   Bourne Co., 1212 Ave. of the Americas, New
              York, NY 10036. (212) 575-1800.

BR   Brodt Music Co., 1409 East Independence Blvd.,
              NC 28201. (704) 332-2177.

BRBR   Broude Bros., 56 West 45th St., New York,
              NY 10036. (212) MU7-4735.

CAP   Composer's Autograph Publications, 1908 Perry
              Ave., Redondo, CA 90278.

CARY   Cary and Co., c/o GI

CF   Carl Fischer, Inc., 62 Cooper Sq., New York,
              NY 10003. (212) 777-0900.

CFP   C. F. Peters Corp., 373 Park Ave. South, New
              York, NY 10016. (212) 686-4147.

CHAP   Chappell and Co. Inc., 810 Seventh Ave., New
              York, NY 10019. (212) 399-7373.

CHES   J. and W. Chester Ltd. , Eagle Court, London
            ECIM 5QD, England, c/o ALB

CON   Concordia Publishing House, 3558 South Jeffer-
            son Ave. , St. Louis, MO 63118. (314) 664-
            7000.

CONCORD   Concord Music Pub. Co. , c/o Henri Elkan, 1316
            Walnut St. , Philadelphia, PA 19107. (215)
            PE5-1900.

CUR   Curwen, c/o GS

DC   Da Capo Press, 227 West 17th St. New York,
            NY 10011. (212) 255-0713.

DIT   Oliver Ditson Co. , c/o TP

DUR   Durand et Cie, c/o TP

EAM   European American Music Distributers Corp. ,
            195 Allwood Road, Clifton, NJ 07012. (201)
            777-2680.

EBM   Edward B. Marks Music Corp. , c/o BEL

ECP   Editions Costallat, Paris, c/o TP

ECS   E. C. Schirmer, Inc. , 112 South St. , Boston,
            MA 02111. (617) 426-3137.

ENOCH   Enoch et Cie, c/o AMP

EME   Editions Max Eschig, Paris, c/o AMP

EVC   Elkan-Vogel Co. Inc. , Presser Place, Bryn
            Mawr, PA 19010, c/o TP

FAB   Faber and Faber, c/o GS

FC   Franco Colombo, c/o BEL

FF   Foetisch Frères, c/o ECS

FLAM   Harold Flammer Inc. , Delaware Water Gap, PA
            18327. (717) 476-0550.

FMC   Frank Music Corp., 1350 Ave. of the Americas, New York, NY 10019. (212) 975-4886.

GAL   Galaxy Music Corp., 2121 Broadway, New York, NY 10023. (212) TR4-2100.

GIA   Gregorian Institute of America, 7404 South Mason Ave., Chicago, IL 60638.

GP   Gregg Press, Westmead, Farenborough, Hants, England.

GRAY   H. W. Gray Co., c/o BEL

GS   G. Schirmer, Inc., 866 Third Ave., New York, NY 10022. (212) 935-5100.

HEU   Heugel et Cie, c/o TP

HF   Harold Flammer, c/o SP

HOPE   Hope Publishing Co., Carol Stream, IL 60187. (312) 665-3200.

HVS   Hannsler Verlag, Stuttgart, c/o CFP

IONE   Ione Press, c/o ECS

JB   Joseph Boonin, Inc., c/o EAM

JF   J. Fischer and Bro., c/o BEL

KAL   Edwin F. Kalmus, 13125 N.W. 47 Ave., Opa Locka, FL 33054. (305) 681-4683.

KIST   Kistner and Siegel, c/o CON

L   Leeds Music Corp., c/o BEL

LC   Leukart Chorblatt, München, c/o AMP

LEM   Henry Lemoine et Cie, c/o TP

LGGS   Lawson-Gould, c/o GS

MB   M. Baron Co., P.O. Box 149, Oyster Bay, NY 11771.

MCA	MCA Music Corp., c/o BEL
MCR	McLaughlin and Reilly Co., c/o SUM
MF	Mark Foster Music Company, Box 4012, Champaign, IL 61820. (207) 367-9932.
MJQ	MJQ Music, Inc., 200 West 57th St., New York, NY 10019. (212) 582-6667.
MM	Mills Music Inc., c/o BEL
MMC	Mercury Music Corp., c/o TP
MP	Music Press, c/o TP
MRF	Musikverlag Rob Forberg, Bad Godesberg, Germany, c/o CFP
MRL	Music Rara, London, c/o TP
MSC	Music Sales Corp., 33 West 60th St., New York, NY 10023. (212) 246-0325.
NOV	Novello and Company, Ltd., 145 Palisade St., Dobbs Ferry, NY 10522. (914) 693-5445.
OX	Oxford University Press, Inc., 200 Madison Ave. New York, NY 10016. (212) 679-7300.
RIC	Ricordi, c/o AMP
RK	Robert King Music Co., 7 Canton St., North Easton, MA 02356.
RONG	Rongwen Music, Inc., c/o BRBR
ROW	Row Music Co., c/o CF
SAL	Editions Salabert, 575 Madison Ave., New York, NY 10022. (212) 486-9230.
SB	Stainer and Bell, c/o GAL
SCHM	Arthur P. Schmidt, c/o SUM
SCH	Schott and Co. Ltd., London, c/o EAM

SIM   Simrock, c/o AMP

SMC   St. Michael's College, Fine Arts Dept. , Winoo-
             ski, VT 05404. (802) 655-2000.

SOM   Somerset, c/o HOPE

SOU   Southern Music Co. (also Peer International
             Corp.), 1740 Broadway, New York, NY   10019.

SP   Shawnee Press, Inc. , Delaware Water Gap, PA
             18327. (717) 476-0550.

SUM   Summy-Birchard Co. , Box CN27, Princeton,
             NJ 09540. (609) 896-1411.

SUP   Editio Supraphon, Prague, c/o BH

SZ   Suvini Zerboni, c/o BH

TP   Theodore Presser Co. , Bryn Mawr, PA   19010.
             (215) 525-3636.

TRANS   Transcontinental Music Publications, 838 Fifth
             Ave. , New York, NY   10021. (212) 249-0100.

UN   Universal Music, c/o EAM

VLD   Verlag Ludwig Doblinger, Wien, c/o AMP

WB   Warner Brothers Music, 9200 Sunset Blvd. , Los
             Angeles, CA   90069. (213) 273-3323.

WIT   Witmark, c/o WB

WL   World Library Publications, 2145 Central Pkwy. ,
             Cincinnati, OH   43214. (513) 421-1090.

WR   Winthrop Rogers Editions, c/o BH

ZAN   Zanibon Edition Co. , c/o CFP

SERVICE AND PROFESSIONAL MUSIC ORGANIZATIONS OF INTEREST TO MALE CHORUS GROUPS

AMERICAN CHORAL DIRECTOR!S ASSOCIATION
Dr. Gene Brooks, National Executive Secretary
P.O. Box 5310, Lawton, OK 73504
(405) 355-8161

AMERICAN CHORAL FOUNDATION, INC.
Sheldon Shoffer, Admin. Dir.
30 W. 56th St., New York, NY 10019
(212) 246-3361

AMERICAN COMPOSERS ALLIANCE
Nicolas Roussakis, Pres.
170 W. 74th St., New York, NY 10023
(212) 362-8900

AMERICAN SOCIETY OF COMPOSERS, AUTHORS AND PUB-
LISHERS (ASCAP)
Stanley Adams, Pres.
1 Lincoln Plaza, New York NY 10023
(212) 595-3050

ASSOCIATED MALE CHORUSES OF AMERICA, INC.
Russell R. Fleharty, Exec.-Sec'y
106 Maplefield Rd.
Pleasant Ridge, MI 48069
(313) 544-1995

BROADCAST MUSIC INC. (BMI)
Edward M. Cramer, Pres. and Chief Exec. Officer
320 W. 57th St., New York, NY 10019
(212) 586-2000

CANADIAN MUSIC CENTRE/CENTRE DE MUSIQUE CAN-
ADIENNE
John Peter Lee Roberts, Dir. Gen.
1263 Bay St., Toronto, Ontario, Canada M5R 2C1
(416) 961-6601

INTERCOLLEGIATE MUSICAL COUNCIL
John Grisby
Department of Music
University of Florida
Gainesville, FL 32603

NATIONAL CHORAL COUNCIL
Martin Josman, Exec. Dir.
250 W. 57th St., New York, NY 10019
(212) 582-0870

SOCIETY FOR THE PRESERVATION AND ENCOURAGEMENT
OF BARBER SHOP QUARTET SINGING IN AMERICA
Hugh A. Ingraham, Exec. Dir.
6315 Third Ave., Kenosha, WI 53140
(414) 654-9111

ALPHABETICAL CATALOG OF MUSIC
FOR MEN'S VOICES

1. ADLER, SAMUEL (1928-). Begin, My Muse. TTBB.
   6 perc. players: xylophone; marimba; 5 tom-toms;
   5 wood blocks; suspended cymbals; drums; vibra-
   phone; snare drum; tambourine; glockenspiel. Eng.
   (1) Love. Text: Anacreon and Anacreonites, Trans.
   Robert Herrick. (2) Brown Penny. Text: W. B.
   Yeats. (3) Lyric. Text: Gil Orlovitz. (4) The
   Eye. Text: Robert Creeley. (5) The Poet Speaks.
   Text: Georgia Douglas Johnson. OX, on rental.
   Composed 1969.

2. ADLER. Two Songs of Hope. (1) Psalm 121 (I Will
   Lift Mine Eyes up to the Mountain). TTBB. org.
   Eng. (2) God is My Salvation. TTBB. org. Eng.
   Text: Isaiah, 12:2, 1, 3-6. MMC #430. Com-
   posed for the Harvard Glee Club in memory of
   Archibald T. Davison.

3. ADLER. Two Views of Love. Unac. (1) As I Lay
   Sleeping. Eng. Text: Anon. (2) Symptoms of
   Love. Eng. Text: Robert Graves. TB #312-
   40979, 80.

4. AICHINGER, GREGOR (1564-1626). Assumpta est
   Maria (Sing to the Lord), arr. McKinney. TTB.
   Unac. Lat. Text: Feast of the Assumption, Second
   Vespers, Antiphon. Eng. Text: Howard McKinney.
   JF #7554. Also AB. (2:00).

5. AICHINGER. Regina Caeli (O Be Joyful), arr. Ruggero

27

Vené. TTBB. Unac. Eng. Text: Harold Heiburg.
BEL #NY 1848.

6. ALTENBURG, MICHAEL (1584-1640). Drei Intraden
(2 for Advent, 1 for Christmas), ed. A. Egidi. (1
and 2) Nun Komm der Heiden Heiland. (3) Wo Gott
der Herr nicht bei uns hält. Unis. 3 vln. va. 2
vc. Ger. Text: originally St. Ambrose, Veni redemptor gentium. CFP 3HV-82.

7. ANDRIESSEN, HENRICK (1892-1964). Missa Fiat Voluntas Tua. TB. Org. Lat. GI #1002.

8. ANDRIESSEN. Missa Sanctus Ludovicus. 3 ev. Unac.
org. Lat. WL.

9. ANDRIESSEN. Missa Sponsa Christi. 3 ev. Unac.
Lat. WL.

10. ANON, 13C. Saturday Lady Mass, ed. Calvin Stapert.
2 pt. male chorus. Unac. OX.

11. ANON, 16C. O Bone Jesu, ed. H. B. Collins. TTBB.
Unac. Lat. CHES.

12. ARCADELT, JACOB (ca. 1505-ca. 1560). Ave Maria,
ed. Frank Damrosch. TTBB. Unac. Lat. GS
#6242. Also, CF #CM 428. Not originally for
men's voices, but well known in this arrangement.

13. ARGENTO, DOMINICK (1927-). The Revelation of
Saint John the Divine, Rhapsody for Tenor, male
chorus, brass and perc. TTBB, extended T solo.
pf. reduction (Brass: 3 hns. F, 2 tr. C, tromb.
2 perc. pf/harp). Eng. Text: St. John. Part I:
Prologue and Adoration. Part 2: The Seven Seals
and Seven Trumpets. Part 3: Jubilation and Epilogue. BH. (36:00).

14. ARNE, THOMAS (1710-1778). Punch (An Emblem of
the Medium of Life), ed. and arr. Marshall Bartholomew. TBB. Unac. Eng. TP #MC150.

15. ARNE. Water parted from the Sea. Unis. pf. Eng.
ECS #1020.

16. ARNOLD, J. H. Magnificat and Nunc Dimittis. Text:
Luke I: 46-56, Luke 2:24-32. TTB. OX #485.

17. ASOLA, GIAMMATTEO (1560-1609). Hoc signum crucis, ed. Fouse. TTBB. Unac. Lat. Text: Feast of the Holy Cross (From 16 Liturgical works by Asola). A-R.

18. ASOLA. Mass in the Eighth Mode. (Missa Octavi Toni), ed. Lindusky. TTBB. Unac. Eng. WL. Also: ed. Bank, AB.

19. ASOLA. Mass Without a Name (Missa Sine Nomine), ed. Eugene Lindusky. TTB (SSA). Unac. Lat. WL #EMO-1138. 3.

20. AVSHALOMOV, JACOB (1919-). Proverbs of Hell. TTBBBB. Narrator. Unac. Eng. Text: William Blake. ACA. Also MCA. (6:00).

21. AZZAIOLO, FILIPPO (16C). My Dear Heart Your Departing (Ti parti, cor mio coro), ed. Don Malin, TTBB. Unac. It. Eng. BEL #OCT 2329. (2:15).

22. BACH, JOHANN SEBASTIAN (1685-1750). There are several tenor-bass duets from the cantatas that are suitable for study and performance (although not originally sung by chorus, they lend themselves to this possibility). Cantata 4, Christ lag in Todesbanden: Mvt. 4, Jesus Christ our God's Own Son. T. (Unis.) 2 vln. cont. Text: Eng. adap. HSD, after Luther. AAC. Also BHW, Ger. (2:15).

23. BACH. Cantata 11, Lobet Gott in seinen Reichen: Mvt. 7, Recitative and Arioso. While Steadfastly They Watched. TB. cont. Text: Eng. adap. HSD. after Acts, 1:10-11. AAC. Also BHW, Ger.

24. BACH. Cantata 33, Allein zu Dir, Herr Jesu Christ: Mvt. 5, Duet: God Whose Very Name is Love. TB. 2 ob. org. cont. Text: Eng. adap. HSD, paraphrase of John 4:8 and Matt. 19:19 (Ger. adap. Johann Schneesing, 1541). AAC. Also BHW, Ger.

25. BACH. Cantata 36, Schwingt freudig euch empor: Mvt. 6, Chorale, Thou the Father Of Us All. T (Unis.). 2 E. hn. cont. Text: Paraphrase of Veni, Redemptor Gentium (Nun komm, der Heiden Heiland) of St. Ambrose, by Luther. Eng. adap. HSD. AAC. Also BHW, Ger.

26.   BACH.   Cantata 44, Sie werden euch in den Bann tun:
      Mvt. 1, Duet, Out From Their Temples. TB. 2
      ob. bn. cont. Text: attr. Christian Weiss, para-
      phrase of John 16:2. Eng. adap. HSD. AAC. Also
      BHW, Ger.

27.   BACH.   Cantata 80, Ein feste Burg ist unser Gott: Mvt.
      5, Chorale, Tho Friends Appear. Unis. 3 tr. timp.
      2 ob. d'amore, str. cont. Text: asc. Luther.
      Eng. adap. HSD. AAC. Also BHW, Ger.

28.   BACH.   Cantata 125, Mit Fried und Freud ich fahr
      dahin: Mvt. 4, Duet, Thruout the Whole Earth.
      TB. 2 vln. cont. Text: atr. Luther, after a
      free rendering of The Song of Simeon (Luke 2:29-
      32). Eng. adap. HSD. AAC. Also BHW, Ger.
      (3:30).

29.   BACH.   Cantata 136, Erforsche mich, Gott: Mvt. 5,
      Duet, We Suffer Sore, by Sin. TB. vln. (Unis.).
      cont. Text: Eng. adap. HSD. AAC. Also BHW,
      Ger.

30.   BACH.   Cantata 140, Wachet auf, ruft, uns die Stimme:
      Mvt. 4, Chorale, Zion Hears The Watchman Call-
      ing. T (Unis). str. cont. Text: Matt. 25:1-13.
      Eng. adap. HSD. AAC. Also BHW, Ger. Fr. Eng.
      (4:00).

31.   BACH.   Cantata 146, Wir müssen durch viel Trübsal:
      Mvt. 2, Duet, O How Will I Glory, TB. 2 ob. str.
      cont. Text: unknown. Eng. adap. HSD. AAC.
      Also BHW, Ger.

32.   BACH.   Cantata 178, Wo Gott, der Herr, nicht bei
      uns hält: Mvt. 4, Tenor Chorale, They Who Would
      Brand Me Heretic. T. (Unis.). 2 ob. d'amore. cont.
      Text: Justus Jonas. Eng. adap. HSD. AAC. Also
      BHW, Ger.

33.   BACH.   Cantata 190, Singet dem Herrn ein neues
      Lied: Mvt. 5, Duet, Jesus Is My All-in-All. TB.
      ob. d'amore. cont. Text: Picander. Eng. adap.
      HSD. Also BHW, Ger.

34.   BACH.   Cantata 196, Der Herr Denket an uns (Wedding
      Cantata), Mvt. 4, Duet, The Lord Prosper You.

TB. org. str. cont. Text: Ps. 115:14. Eng.
adap. HSD. AAC. Also BHW, Ger. Also: CFP
#6079, ed. A. Mendel.

35. BACH. Easter Oratorio: Kommt, eilet und Laufet.
Duet, TB. 2 tromb. 2 ob. str. cont. Text: Picander. KAL.

36. BACON, ERNST (1898-   ). Bennington Riflemen. A
two part setting (not arranged) with pf. acc. SA,
TB or two soloists. Eng. BH #5931.

37. BACON. Buttermilk Hill. TB. pf. Both Buttermilk
Hill and Riflemen were Bicentennial pieces written
for the El Cerrito Public Schools of Richmond, California. Buttermilk has opt. instruments: vln. fl.
rec. bells, small drum or tamb. BH #5944.

38. BACON. Seven Canons. 2-4 ev. pf. Eng. (1) God.
Text: Angelus Silesius, trans. Paul Carus. (2)
Sinai. Text: Talmud. (3) Schools and Rules.
Text: William Blake. (4) The Pelican. Text:
unknown. (5) The Little Children. Text: Talmud.
(6) Chop-Cherry. Text: Robert Herrick. (7)
Money. Text: unknown. MMC #352-00114.

39. BALLANTINE, EDWARD (1886-1971). The House
Among the Trees, Stockbridge. TTBB. pf. Eng.
Text: J. L. McLane, Jr. ESC. #65.

40. BANTOCK, GRANVILLE (1868-1946). Midnight Epilogue from Asolanda. TTBB. Unac. Eng. ENOCH.

41. BANTOCK. She Walks in Beauty. TTBB. Unac. Eng.
Text: Byron. NOV #656.

42. BANTOCK. Silent Strings. TTBB. pf. Eng. Text:
Helen Taylor. BH #1455. (2:15).

43. BANTOCK. Vision of Belshazzar. TTBB. Unac.
Text: Byron. MM #80247.

44. BARBER, SAMUEL (1910-   ). A Nun Takes the Veil.
TTBB. Unac. Eng. Text: Gerard Manley Hop-
kins. GS #10859. (1:30).

45. BARBER. A Stopwatch and an Ordnance Map. Com-

posed in 1945. TTBB. (some div.). 3 timp. T.
and B. solos. Eng. Text: Stephen Spender. GS
#8799. (5:30). (parts for optional accompaniment:
4 hns. 3 tromb. tuba, available on rental.) First
performance by the Collegiate Chorale, Robert
Shaw, Cond.

46. BARLOW, WAYNE (1912-). Diversify the Abyss.
TTBB. pf. Eng. Text: Hyam Plutzik. TP #312-
40570. Composed 1963.

47. BARROW, ROBERT (1911-). Christians, Awake,
Salute the Happy Morn. TTBB. org. Eng. ECS #2173.

48. BARROW. Hush My Dear, Lie Still and Slumber.
TTBB. Unac. Eng. Text: Isaac Watts. ECS
#2173. Composed 1961.

49. BARROW. Three Psalms of Penitence. (1) Out of
the Deep, Ps. 130. (2) Bow Down Thine Ear, Ps.
86. (3) Show Me Thy Ways, O Lord, Ps. 25.
TTBB. org. or str. Eng. Texts: Psalms. Unpublished. Available from CAP.

50. BARTOK, BELA (1881-1945). Five Slovak Folk Songs.
TTBB. Unac. Text: Slovak-Hungarian Folk. Eng.
Trans. Nancy Busch. Ger. trans. Mirko Jelusich.
Hung. trans. Wanda Gleiman. BH #17682. (6:30).
Composed in 1917.

51. BARTOK. Four Old Hungarian Folk Songs. TTBB.
Unac. Eng. trans. Matyas Seiber and Leo Black.
BH #5575. (6:00). Composed in 1912.

52. BASSETT, LESLIE (1923-). Prayers for Divine Service. TTBB. Unac. Lat. In 3 mvts. (1) Mun-
da cor meum. (2) Domine Jesu Christe. (3) Agnus
Dei. Composed in 1965 for Williams College. ACA.

53. BECK, JOHN NESS (1930-). A New Heart Will I
Give You. TTBB. pf/org. Eng. Text: adopted
from Ezeckiel. GS #11781.

54. BECKER, JOHN (1886-1961). Mass in Unison or Two
Parts, in the Gregorian Manner. Lat. ACA.

55. BECKER. Missa Symphonica. TTBB. Unac. Lat.
Mass Texts. ACA.

56. BEESON, JACK (1921-   ). Everyman's Handyman.
    9 rounds and canons for men's voices: (1) To
    Cure a Kicking Cow. (2) To Prevent Flies from
    Injuring Picture Frames. (3) Against Taking Poison
    Accidentally. (4) Against Falling Asleep in Church.
    (5) To Remove Moles and Warts. (6) Potatoes as
    Paste and Pen-Wipers. (7) To Rid Yourself of
    Rats with Poison. (8) An Excellent Cement. (9)
    To Revive a Chilled Pig. Unac. Eng. Text: Eliz-
    abeth W. Smith. BH #5817.

57. BEESON. In Praise of Bloomers. TTBB. Unac.
    Eng. Text: Anon. BH #5754.

58. BEESON. The Bear Hunt (or: The Triumph of Feist,
    The Hound-Dog). TBB. pf. Eng. Text: adapted
    from Abraham Lincoln. MM.

59. BEETHOVEN, LUDWIG VAN (1770-1827). O welche
    Lust; Fidelio, ed. Rhodes. TTBB. pf. T.B.
    solos. Ger. Text: Schikaneder. Eng. trans.
    W. Rhodes. CF #CM2245. Also GS#1169. (3:30).

60. BEETHOVEN. Song of Farewell. TT(B)B. Unac.
    Text: Ger. Jos. Ritter van Seyfried. Eng. Trans.
    adap. HSD. AAC.

61. BEETHOVEN. William Tell: Song of the Monks (Swift in
    Its Course Comes Death to Man). TTB. Unac. Text:
    Ger. Schiller. Eng. trans. and adap. HSD. AAC. #28.

62. BELLINI, VINCENZO (1801-1835). Norma: Coro di
    guerrieri (Non parti? Finora è al campo), Act II,
    sc. 4. TTB. pf. It. Also, sc. 5 is possible:
    TTB, B. solo Text: Felice Romani. RIC. (4:00).

63. BENDER, JAN (1909-   ). Anthems for TB (SA). org.
    Eng. (1) He Who Is Not With Me Is Against Me.
    CON. #98-2058. (2) Peace Be With You. CON.
    #98-2086. (3) Three Prophecies, op. 32, no. 25.
    CON. #98-2133. Text: Matthew 2:13-23 (Gospel
    for Sunday after New Year). (4) Unless One is
    Born Anew. CON. #98-2056. (5) When the Coun-
    selor Comes. CON. #98-2055. (6) You Wicked
    Servant. CON. #98-2085.

64. BENDER. Gospel Motets, op. 32. All for 2 ev. org.
    Eng. (1) Begone Satan, from the Gospel, First

34   Music for Men's Voices

Sunday in Lent. Text: Matt. 15:4-10. (2) Come,
O Blessed of my Father, Trinity 26. Text: Matt.
15:25-34. (3) It is not Fair, second Sunday in
Lent. Text: Matt. 15:26-28. (4) Lord, Lord,
Open to Us, Trinity 26. Text: Matt. 25:11-13.
(5) Sir, Come Down Before My Child Dies, Trinity 21. Text: John 4:45-50. CON #98-1848;
#98-1833; #98-1834, #98-1835.

65. BENJAMIN, ARTHUR (1893-1960). To a Wine Jug.
TTBB. pf. Eng. Text: Anon. Greek, trans.
A.C. Benson. BH #5249.

66. BENNETT, RICHARD RODNEY (1936-). The House
of Sleepe. 6 voices. Text: from Ovid's Meta-
morphosen. Trans. to Eng. by Arthur Gulding
and John Gower. UE (12:00).

67. BENSON, WARREN (1924-). God Rest Ye Merry
Gentlemen. TB. pf. Eng. CF. (2:00).

68. BENSON. Lotus of the True Law. TTBB. opt. perc.
Eng. CF. (7:00).

69. BERGER, JEAN (1909-). Doublets. (1) Let's Im-
itate the Horse. TTBB (SSAA). 2 fl., stb. Tambourine, cymbals. EV #362-03148.

70. BERGER. Hope for Tomorrow. TTBB. pf. Eng.
Text: Martin Luther King, Jr. GS #10717.

71. BERGER. I've known Rivers. TTBB. Unac. Eng.
Text: Langston Hughes. ROW #158. (5:30).
Based on a poem, The Negro Speaks of Rivers
from the Dream Keeper, by Langston Hughes.

72. BERGER. Old Moby Dick. TTBB. pf. Eng. Text:
W. Storrs Lee, ROW #532. (3:00).

73. BERGER. She'd Be Good If She Could But She Can't.
TTBB. pf. Eng. Text: W. Storrs Lee. ROW
#533. (2:15).

74. BERGER. Three Fancies: (1) The Bounty of Our Age.
(2) On a Spark of Fire Fixing on a Gentlewoman's
Breast. (3) If all the World Were Paper. TTBB.
pf. Eng. Texts: (1) Farley, 1621. (2) Philipott,
1641. (3) Anon. 1641. ROW #517.

75. BERGSMA, WILLIAM (1921-). Let True Love
    Among Us Be. TB. pf. Eng. Text: 13th Cent.
    Eng. Sacred Anon. modern text by Nancy Nicker-
    son. CF #CM6534. (2:00). Composed 1950.

76. BERKELEY, LENNOX (1903-). Ask Me No More.
    TTBB. Unac. Eng. Text: Thomas Carew. CHES
    #JWC 8783. Composed 1950.

77. BERKELEY. Salve Regina. Unis. org. Lat. CHES
    #JWC 4725.

78. BERKELEY. Three Songs for Four Male Voices.
    TTBB. Unac. Eng. (1) Fair Daffodils. Text:
    Herrick. (2) Spring Goeth All in White. Text:
    Bridges. (3) Kissing Usurie. Text: Herrick.
    Commissioned by the University of California at
    Santa Barbara, 1965. CHES.

79. BERLIOZ, HECTOR (1803-1869). Le Chant des Bre-
    tons, ed. Erich Kunzel. TTBB. pf. Fr. Eng.
    Text: Julian A. P. Brizeaux. This was published
    in two revisions, 1835 and 1850. The second was
    titled Fleurs des Landes. BH #5401.

80. BERLIOZ. Choruses from the Damnation of Faust.
    (Soldiers Chorus and Students Chorus). Voice
    parts modified and arr. by Clough-Leighter. TTBB.
    pf. Fr. Text: Goethe. Eng. trans. Henry Chor-
    ley. ECS #565. Also: two other sections; Sc. VI,
    Chouer de Buveurs (Oh, qu'il fait bon) and Fugue,
    Sur le Thème de Brander--Amen.

81. BERLIOZ. L'Enfance du Christ; Chorus of Magicians,
    Part I, scene IV. TTBB. pf. B. solo. Fr. Text:
    Berlioz. Eng. John Bernhoff. GS. (4:15).

82. BERLIOZ. Requiem. Lat. Text: Requiem Mass.
    (1) Quid sum Miser. TTB. (3:15). (2) Hostias.
    TTBB. (3:00). (3) Agnus Dei. TTBB. (4:00).
    GS.

83. BERLIOZ. Serenade of the Capulets (Ohé, Capulets,
    Bonsoir); Romeo and Juliet, op. 17. TBB-TBB.
    pf. Fr. Text: E. Deschamps, Eng. trans. John
    Bernhoff. KAL. (1:15).

84. BERNSTEIN, LEONARD (1918-). Pirate Song: Pet-

er Pan. TTBB. Bar. solo. pf. Eng. Text:
Bernstein. GS #9915.

85. BETTS, LORNE (1918-). Joe Harris 1913-1942.
     TTBB. Male narrator. pf/orch: 2222/2220/perc.
     Eng. Text: Earle Birney. (20:00). MS. avail-
     able from Canadian Music Centre. Composed 1950.

86. BEVERIDGE, THOMAS (1938-). Drop, Drop, Slow
     Tears. TTBB. pf. Eng. Text: Phineas Fletcher.
     ECS #2174.

87. BEVERIDGE. Songs of Praise (13 Hymns and Re-
     sponses for Equal Voices). TTB (SSA). Eng.
     ECS #2560.

88. BINCHOIS, GILLES DE (ca. 1400-1440). A solus or-
     tus cardine, ed. Paul Boepple. TBB (SSA). Unac.
     Lat. Text: Caelius Sedulius. MP #38. (4:00).

89. BINKERD, GORDON (1916-). Binkerd is one of the
     few American Indian composers. He was born on
     Ponce Indian Reservation in Lynch, Nebraska.
     Studies were with Piston at Harvard and Rogers at
     Eastman. He has composed extensively for male
     voices. BINKERD. Alleluia for St. Francis. TB
     (SA). Org. Eng. Text: from the Roman--Sephardic
     Hymnal. BH #5686.

90. BINKERD. And Viva Sweet Love. TBB. pf. 4 hands.
     Eng. Text: e.e. Cummings. BH #5750. (5:00).

91. BINKERD. A Scotch Mist (free working "arrange-
     ments" of Scotch airs). (1) Wilt Thou Be My Dear-
     ie. TBB. (2) Clout the Caudron. TTBB. (3)
     Ay Wauking. TBB. Scots glossary provided where
     needed. BH.

92. BINKERD. Dum medium silentium TTBB. Unac. Lat.
     Text: Wisdom 18:14, 15. (Introit, Sunday within
     the Octave of Christmas). BH #5630. (4:00).

93. BINKERD. Feast of St. Francis of Assisi (Gradual
     and Alleluia). TB (SA). org. Eng. Text: Ps.
     36:30-31. BH #5827.

94. BINKERD. From Your Throne, O Lord. Unis. org.

Eng. Text: Ps. 79:2 (3rd Sunday of Advent). BH
#5826.

95. BINKERD. Let My Prayer Come Like Incense. TB.
org. Eng. Text: Ps. 140:2 (Gradual, 19th Sunday
after Pentecost). BH #5828.

96. BINKERD. Liebeslied (The Song of Love). TTBB.
Unac. Ger. Text: Rainer Maria Rilke. Eng. Ludwig Lewisohn. BH #5631. (4:00).

97. BINKERD. Songs from the Silver Tassie. TBB. pf.
Eng. Text: Sean O'Casey. BH #5830.

98/99. BINKERD. They Lie at Rest. TTBB. Unac. Eng.
Text: Christina Rossetti (Songs for Strangers and
Pilgrims). Music based on the hymn tune "Melita"
by J. B. Sykes and "All mein Gedanken" from the
Lochheimer Leiderbuch, ca. 1450. BH #5954.

100. BINKERD. Through Your Strangeness Frets My
Heart. TTBB. Unac. Text: Thomas Campion.
BH.

101. BIZET, GEORGES (1838-1875). Carmen: Act I,
Sur la Place. TB. B. Solo. French. Text:
Meilhac and Halevy. GS. (2:00).

102. BIZET. Saint John of Pathmos, op. 14 (Hear ye all,
I am John). TBB. Eng. trans. George Osgood
(orig. text, Victor Hugo). BMC #149.

103. BLISS, SIR ARTHUR (1891-1975). Two Songs from
the film: The Beggar's Opera (1935), arr. Bliss.
TTBB. pf. Eng. Text: words varied by Christopher Fry; melody from the March in Rinaldo, Handel. (1) Let Us Take the Road. (2) Fill Every
Glass. NOV #703.

104. BLISS, MILTON (1927-). The Tower of Babel.
TTBB. pf. Eng. Text: Genesis 11:1-9. BRBR.

105. BLITZSTEIN, MARC (1905-1964). Invitation to Bitter-
ness. TTBB. pf. Eng. Text: Blitzstein. AR-
ROW. (3:00). Composed 1939.

106. BLITZSTEIN. The Airborne (symphony) for male

chorus and orch: 3343/4331 perc. pf. cel. hp/str.
Eng. CHAP.

107. BLOW, LEO (1878- ?). Shivisi, op. 4. TTBB.
Unac. Heb. (From Cantorial Anthology. Vol. 4,
ed. Ephros). Text: Hebrew Liturgy. BLOCH.

108. BOURGEOIS, LOUIS (ca. 1510-1561?). Two Evening
Hymns: A Gladsome Light and Darkening Night,
arr. C. F. Simkins, harm. Claude Goudimel.
TTBB. Unac. Texts: Greek, 3rd Cent. Eng.
trans. Robert Bridges. OX #214.

109. BRAHMS, JOHANNES (1833-1897). Five Songs for
Male Chorus (Fünf Soldatenlieder) op. 41, ed.
Leonard de Paur. TTB. Unac. Ger. Text: Carl
Lemke. Eng. Text: de Paur. (1) My Horn Shall
Sound in Trouble's Vale (Ich schwing mein Horn).
(2) All Volunteers Come (Freiwillige her!). (3)
The Last Escort (Geleit). (4) Marching (Marschie-
ren). (5) Take Care (Gebt acht). LGGS #51450.
(17:00).

110. BRAHMS. Rinaldo, op. 50. TTBB. pf. Orig.
Orch. 2(P)22/2223/Timp/str. Text: Goethe. Eng.
trans. HSD. AAC #10. (45:00). Composed 1863/
68. There is a recording of "Rinaldo" by The Am-
brosian Chorus and New Philharmonia Orch. London #OS26106. (40:00).

111. BRAHMS. Liebeslieder Waltzer, op. 52 (Love Waltz-
es), ed. Shaw. pf. 4 hands. Ger. Eng. Suitable
for chorus: (3) O die Frauen, TB. (1:15). (14)
Sieh, wie ist die Welle klar, TB. (1:15). (17)
Nichwandle, T. (2:15). Text: Georg Friedrich
Daumer. LGGS #834.

112. BRAHMS. Alto Rhapsody, op. 53. TTBB. org. A.
solo. orig. orch: 2222/2000/str. Text: Goethe,
Harzreise im Winter. Eng. trans. John Moment.
JP #8559. (13:00). Composed 1869.

113. BRAHMS. Neue Liebeslieder Waltzer, op. 65. pf.
4 hands. Ger. Following suitable for chorus: (No.
4) Ihr Schwarzen Augen. (B); (0:50). (No. 10) Ich
kose süss (T); (0:50). Text: Georg Friedrich Daumer. Eng. Natalia Mac Farren. SIM.

114. BRITTEN, BENJAMIN (1913-1976). Rustics and
     Fisherman; Gloriana. TTBB. Unac. Eng. Text:
     W. Plomer. BH #5017.

115. BRITTEN. The Ballad of Little Musgrave and Lady
     Barnard. TBB. pf. Eng. Text: Anon. Oxford
     Book of Ballads. BH #1992. (12:00). Composed
     1943.

116. BRITTEN. Variation II, "Herod" from A Boy was
     Born. (pp. 18-32 of piano-vocal score). Eng.
     Text: Anon. before 1529. Composed 1932-1933.
     OX.

117. BRUCH, MAX (1838-1920). Bruch's male choral
     music is largely undiscovered. Although some
     foreign importation is necessary, they are well
     worth looking into. Of particular interest is Frith-
     jof, op. 23. TTBB./orch: 2222/4301 harp. Timp/
     str. KIST. In 5 scenes. (45:00). Composed
     1864. Also GS #5530.

118. BRUCH. Normannenzug, op. 32. Unis. men, B.
     solo. orch: 2222/4230/timp/str. BHL/BHW.

119. BRUCH. Vom Rhein. Men's chorus. Unac. KIST.

120. BRUCH. Media vita (Battle-hymn of the Monks).
     Ger. Scheffel. Eng. trans. Frances Holden Seaver.
     GS #4820.

121. BRUCH. Totenfeier; Vergiss, O Seele, nicht die
     Toten op. 89. Men's chorus. Unac/org/3 tromb,
     tuba/3 tr., 3 tromb., 2 tubas, timp/org. and wds.
     LC.

122. BRUCKNER, ANTON (1824-1896). Abendzauber.
     TTBB. 4 hns. T(B) solo (and three yodelers off
     stage). UN #2194.

123. BRUCKNER. Am Grabe, ed. Grote. TTBB. Unac. Ger.
     SCHOTT. (4:00).

124. BRUCKNER. Ave Maria. TTBB-TTBB. Unac. Lat.
     Text: Luke 1:28. ARIS #AE112. (3:45).

125. BRUCKNER. The Noblest of Songs (Das Deutsche

Lied), ed. J. Park. TTBB. pf. Eng. Ger. Text:
Erich Fels. BR #VF2. (3:00). Composed 1892.
Orig. orch: 4 hns. 3 tr. 3 tromb. B. Tuba.

126. BRUCKNER. Fest-Cantate, ed. Karl Etti. TTBB.
TTBB. Unac. Lat. Orch. reduced for pf. Ger.
Text: Max Prammersburger. VLD. Orch: 2222/
4231/timp.

127. BRUCKNER. Helgoland. TTBB. Orch: 2222/4331/
timp/str. Ger. Text: August Silberstein. BAR
#AE263. (16:00). Composed 1893.

128. BRUCKNER. Inveni David TTBB. 2 tromb. ad lib.
Lat. Text: Ps. 89:20-21. (Gradual, Mass of a
Martyr-Bishop). CFP #6318.

129. BRUCKNER. Locus iste, ed. Linshinsky. TTBB.
Unac. Lat. Text: Gradual, Dedication of a Church.
ARIS #AE155.

130. BRUCKNER. Trösterin Musik. TTBB. Unac/org.
Ger. Text: A. Seuffert. UN #UE3294. (4:00).
Written in 1877. Orig. orch: 2222/4231/timp./
str.

131. BRUCKNER. Um Mitternacht (At Midnight). TTBB.
A. solo. Unac. Ger. Text: R. Prutz. UN #UE3292.
(5:00). Composed 1864.

132. BRUMEL. Mater patris et filia, ed. Elliot Forbes.
TBB. Unac. Lat. Text: Unknown. "This motet
is one of the few 15C compositions written specifically for men's voices," Forbes. GS #11011. Also AB.

133. BUCK, DUDLEY (1839-1909). In Absence. TTBB.
Unac. Eng. NOV #45 0763 00.

134. BUCK. On The Sea. TTBB. Unac. Eng. GS
#1022.

135. BULLOCK, ERNEST (1890-). Give Us the Wings
of Faith (Saints Day Anthem). TB. org. Eng.
Text: Isaac Watts. OX #A151.

136. BURLEIGH, HARRY T. (1866-1949). Mother O'Mine.

TTBB. Unac. Eng. Text: Rudyard Kipling. RIC
#106033.

137. BUSONI, FERRUCCIO (1866-1924). Concerto in C
Major for Piano and Orchestra with final chorus
for Male Chorus, op. 39. Text: Hymn to Pillah,
from the play Alladin, Oehlenschlager. pub. Breitkopf. (68:00). Orch: 4444/4432/str.

138. BUSONI. Vier Männerchöre, op. 40. (Primavera,
Estate, Autunno, Inverno). RIC. Composed 1882.

139. BUSSOTTI, SYLVANO (1931-). Siciliano. 12 male
voices. Unac. A chance composition. Pub. by
Aldo Bruzzichelli, Florence.

140. BUXTEHUDE, DIETRICH (1637-1707). Sion hört die
Wächter Singen (Zion Hears the Watchman Singing),
ed. H. Clough-Leighter. TB. org. (pf.) Ger.
Text: Matt. 25:1-13. trans. Katherine Winkworth,
ECS #538.

141. BYRD, WILLIAM (1542-1623). Lord, in Thy Rage
(Domine in furore): from Songs of Sundrie Natures.
TTB. Unac. Eng. Text: Ps. 6. AMP #NYPM5.
(2:00).

142. BYRD. Mass in Three Parts. (Missa Sine Nomine),
ed. Manzetti. TTB. Unac. Lat. MCR #1385.
Also AB. (20:30).

143. CADMAN, CHARLES WAKEFIELD (1881-1946). Con-
ceited. TTBB. Opt. solos. pf. Eng. CONCORD.
#C-22-17.

144. CANNING, THOMAS (1911-). The Temptation of
Jesus. TTBB. Narrator. 2 hns. 2 tr, 3 tromb.,
Tuba, perc. ACA.

145. CAPLET, ANDRE (1875-1925). Messe à Trois Voix.
Unac. Lat. DUR. (20:00).

CARTER, ELLIOTT (1908-). Carter has written
three choral works for, and dedicated to, The Harvard Glee Club: Emblems, Defense of Corinth
and Tarantella.

146. CARTER. Emblems. TTBB. pf. Eng. Text:
      Allen Tate. MMC #MP 120. (16:00). Composed
      1947.

147. CARTER. Tarantella. TTBB. pf. (4 hands). Eng.
      Text: Latin of Ovid. AMP. Composed 1937.

148. CARTER. The Defense of Corinth. (When Philip
      King of Macedon enterprised the seige and ruin of
      Corinth). TTBB. speaker. pf. 4 hands. Eng.
      Text: Rabelais. MMC #54. (17:00). Composed
      1941.

149. CASALS, PABLO (1876-1973). Nigra sum (I Am
      Black). TTB. pf. org. Lat. Text: Eng. vers.
      Kenneth Sterne. ALB #240-8. (5:00). Not origin-
      ally for men's voices.

150. CAUSTON, THOMAS (-1569). Rejoice in the
      Lord, ed. H. Panteleoni. TTBB. Unac. Eng.
      Text: Phil. 4:4-7. CON #98-1534.

151. CAVALLI, PIETRO FRANCESCO (1602-1676). Three
      Hymns, realized by Raymond Leppard. (1) Iste
      confessor. TT. 2 vln. cont. (2) Ave maris
      stella and (3) Deus tuorum militum TTBB. 2 vln.
      cont. Text: (1) Iste, attr. Rabanus Maurus. (2)
      Ave maris, attr. Fortunatus. (3) Deus tuorum,
      Anon. 6th Cent. FAB. (4:30 ea.).

152. CERTON, PIERRE (1510-1572). J'ay le rebours
      (chanson), ed. Elliot Forbes. TTBB. Unac. Fr.
      ECS #2323.

153. CHAMPAGNE, CLAUDE (1891-1965). Ave Maria.
      TTBB. Unac. Lat. Text: Luke 1:28. BMI-C
      #182. (2:00).

154. CHAMPAGNE. Missa Brevis à Trois Voix. Unac.
      Lat. BMI-C.

155. CHARPENTIER, MARC ANTOINE (1634-1704). Lau-
      date Dominum, ed. H. Wiley Hitchcock. TTB.
      org. Lat. Text: Ps. 116, EBM MG 4603. (4:15).
      Also for 2 vln, org./pf.

156. CHARPENTIER. Magnificat. TTB. 2 vln. vc. key-

board. (original: Hautecontre, Tenor, Bass).
Lat. Text: Luke 1:46-56. FF. (10:00).

157. CHERUBINI, LUIGI (1760-1842). Requiem in D Minor.
TTB. orch. score reduced for pf. Lat. CFP.
#51. (45:00) KAL #6140. Orch: 2222/2230/timp/
str.

158. CHIMARA, PAUL (1938-). Ave Maria--Scarborough
Fair. TTBBBB. Unac. Lat. CFP #P66564. (4:00).

159. CLARKE, HENRY L. (1895-). Dona Nobis Pacem.
TTBB. Unac. Lat. ACA.

160. CLARKE. O Wild West Wind. TTBB. Unac. Eng.
Text: Shelley. ACA.

161. CLARKE. Sanctus from St. Cecilia's Day. TBB
(SSS). org. Lat. ACA.

162. CLEMENT, JACQUES (ca. 1510-1556?). (Also known
as Clemens non Papa). Adoramus Te, ed. Davison.
TTBB. Unac. Lat. Text: asc. St. Francis of
Assisi. ECS #948.

163. CLOKEY, JOSEPH (1890-1960). Holiday Cruise,
choral cycle for TTBB. pf. Eng. Text: Willis
Knapp Jones. (1) An Invitation. CF #9053; (2)
The Departure, CF #9054; (3) Dawn at Sea, CF
#9055; (4) The Cloud Ship. CF #9056.

164. CLOKEY. Souvenir. TTBB. Unac. Eng. Text:
Clayton C. Quest. CF #6119.

165. COCCHI, GIOACCHINO (1715-1804). Colla bottiglia
in mano, ed. David Randolph. TTBB. Unac. It.
Text: Unknown. LGGS.

166. CONVERSE, FREDERICK (1871-1940). Laudate Dominum. TTBB. 2 tr. F, 3 T. tromb. and B. tromb.
ad lib. org. (possible to play only with org.). Lat.
Text: Ps. 148. BMC #228.

167. COPLAND, AARON (1900-). Old American Songs,
Set 1 (adapted by Copland, Wilding-White, Fine).
(1) The Boatmen's Dance. TTBB. pf. Eng. Text:
Minstrel-Folk Song, 1843. BH #1908. (4:00).

(2) The Dodger. TTBB. pf. Eng. Text: American-
Folk Campaign Song. BH #1909. (1:30). (3)
Simple Gifts. TB. pf. Eng. Text: American-
Folk Shaker. BH #1903. (1:30). (4) I Bought Me
a Cat. TBB. pf. Eng. Text: Children's Folk
Song. BH #1910. (3:00).

168. COPLAND. Old American Songs, Set 2 (adapted by
Copland, Wilding-White, Fine). (1) The Little
Horses (lullaby). TTBB. pf. Eng. Text: American
Folk. BH #5510. (3:00). (2) At the River.
TTBB. pf. Eng. Text: American Folk. BH
#5514. (3:30). (3) Ching-a-ring Chaw. TTBB.
Eng. pf. Text: Minstrel-Folk Song. BH #5518.
(1:30).

169. COPLAND. Song of the Guerrillas from the film:
The North Star. TBB. B. solo. pf. Eng. Text:
Ira Gershwin. BH #1729. (4:00).

170. COPLAND. Stomp Your Foot from the Tender Land,
arr. by the composer for TTBB. pf. duet. Eng.
Text: Horace Everett. BH #5136. (3:00).

171. CORNELIUS, PETER (1824-1874). Ach, Wie Nichtig,
Ach, Wie Fluchtig, op. 9, no. 1. TTBB, A.
solo. Unac. SCH #C38. 536.

172. CORNELIUS. Der Alte Soldat. 9 pt. men's chorus.
Unac. Ger. BHW. Also NOV #Orph. 382 Eng.

173. CORNELIUS. Requiem aeternam (Calm Repose Eternal), ed. Clifford G. Richter. TTBB. Unac. Lat.
Eng. Text: Requiem Mass. ALB #814-5. (2:25).

174. CORNYSH, WILLIAM (-1523). Ave Maria and
Gaude Virgo, ed. Frank L. Harrison. These are
taken from Vols. X and XIII of MUSICA BRITAN-
NICA. SB.

175. COUTURE, JEAN PAPINEAU (1916-). Laudate
eum; Psalm 150. TTBB. 3 tr. 3 tromb. org.
Lat. BMC-C. (3:00).

176. COUTURE. Te mater alma. TTBB. Unac. Lat.
Text: Anon. Lauds Hymn. SMC. (1:30).

177. COWELL, HENRY (1897-1965). A Thanksgiving

Psalm: from the Dead Sea Scrolls. TTTBBB.
Orch: 2 tr. B-flat, 2 hns. 2 fl. 2 ob. 2 cl.
B-flat, 2 bn. timp. str. Eng. trans. Millar Bur-
rows. AMP, on rental.

178. COWELL. Day, Evening, Night, Morning. TTBBB
(2 part falsetto or boys' voices, ad lib.). Unac.
Eng. Text, Paul Laurence Dunbar. SOU
#ME1001. (12:00). Composed 1950.

179. COWELL. Evening at Brookside. TTBB, T. solo.
Unac. Eng. Text: Harry Cowell. SOU #ME1002.
(4:00). Composed 1950.

180. COWELL. Luther's Carol for His Son. TTBB. Unac. Eng. Text: James, John and Robert Wedder-
burn (from Ane Compendium Buik of Godly and
Spiritual Sanges, 1567). L #L-237. (3:00).

181. COWELL. Supplication. Unis. 2 tr. 2 tromb.
timp. ad lib. Eng. Text: Cowell. CFP #6322.
(3:30). Composed 1962.

182. CRAWFORD, JOHN (1931-). Amour, Tu as été
mon Maître (Four Settings). TTB. Unac. Fr.
Eng. (1) I Have Lost All That Once I Was. (De
soi-même). Text: Clément Marot. (2) The Fair-
est Maid (Je suis aimé de la plus belle). Text:
Marot. (3) Here Is the God Who Looks Both Ways
(Voici le Père au double front). Text: du Bellay.
(4) All That Has Life and Beauty (Tout ce qui prend
naissance). Text: du Bellay. ECS #2176, 2177,
2178, 2179.

183. CRAWFORD. Psalm 98. TBB. pf. brass. Eng.
Text: Ps. 98. OX.

184. CRESTON, PAUL (1906-). Here Is Thy Footstool,
op. 11. TTBB. Unac. Eng. Text: Tagore. GS
#9793. (2:45). Composed 1945.

185. CRESTON. Missa Adoro Te. TB. org. Lat. JF
#8751. (18:00).

186. CRESTON. Missa Solemnis, op. 44. TTBB. (or
SATB). org. orch. parts on rental. Lat. MM.
(20:00). There is also an SATB version by the
composer. Composed 1964.

187. CRESTON. The Celestial Vision, op. 60. TTBB.
      Unac. Eng. Texts: Dante, Whitman, Arjuna. (Ar-
      juna trans. Eng. Sir Edward Arnold). SP. (9:00).
      Creston's real name is Joseph Guttovegio.

188. CRESTON. Thou Hast Made Me Endless; Three
      Chorales from Tagore, op. 11. TTBB. Unac.
      Eng. Text: Tagore. (No. 1. SSAA; No. 3, SATB).
      GS #9792. Composed 1945.

189. CRESTON. Two Motets, op. 45; Adoro Te and Salve
      Regina. TTBB. org. Lat. Eng. Adoro Te: B.
      solo. Text: St. Thomas Aquinas. Salve: T.
      solo. Text: attr. Hermannus Contractus. GC
      #9912. (6:00).

190. CROCE, GIOVANNI (1557-1609). Ego sum pauper,
      ed. Rev. Walter Williams. TTBB. Unac. Lat.
      Text: Ps. 69:30, 31. Eng. Williams. ECS #698.

191. CRUTCH, WILLIAM (1775-1847). Come, Praise the
      Lord. TBB. pf. Eng. CON.

192. CRUFT, ADRIAN (1921-). Two Anthems, op. 20.
      (1) May God Abide. TTBB. Unac. Eng. Text:
      John 4:16. (1:30). (2) Thy God was Making Haste.
      TTBB. Unac. Eng. Text: Richard Crashaw.
      SB35667.

193. CRUGER, J. and F. MENDELSSOHN. Now Thank
      We All Our God, ed. and arr. A. Hilton. TTBB.
      opt. brass quartet. TP #MC371.

194. CRUVELLI, G. B. Ut flos, et rosa, ed. Jerome Roche.
      TT. Keyboard. OX.

195. DALLA PICCOLA, LUIGI (1904-1975). Estate (Sum-
      mer). TTBB. Text from a fragment of Alceo, in
      It. by E. Romagnoli. ZAN #2856. (4:00). Com-
      posed 1932.

196. DALLA PICCOLA. La Canzone del Quarnaro. TTBB,
      T. solo. Orch: 3333/6331/Timp. 2 hps. pf.
      perc./str. It. Text: Gabriele D'Annunzio. MS
      (BH). (15:00).

197. DAVIDSON, HAROLD (1908-). A Collection of Corny
      Gems. TTBB. Unac. Text: Davidson. WB #9-3239.

198. DAVIDSON. A Collection of Sad but True Ballads.
      TTBB. Unac. Eng. Text: Davidson. WB #9-3239.

199. DAVIDSON. A Collection of Silly but Sad Ballads.
      TTBB. Unac. Eng. Text: Davidson. WB #9-
      R3238.

200. DAVIES, PETER MAXWELL (1934-). Alma Re-
      demptoris Mater. 4 ev. From Four Christmas
      Carols on Medieval Texts. SCH.

201. DAVIS, KATHERINE K. (1892-). Come Ye to
      Bethlehem. TTBB. Unac. pf/org. Eng. Text:
      John Cowley. Trad. Eng. air freely arranged.

202. DAVIS. The Firmament of Power. TTBB. Unac.
      Eng. Ps. 150, 149, 145. WB #3797.

203. DAVIS. The Humble Shepherds. TTBB (SSAA). Un-
      ac. Eng. Text: Rhys Williams. BMC #2197.

204. DEBUSSY, CLAUDE (1862-1918). Invocation. TTBB.
      pf. T. solo. Fr. Text: Alphonse de Lamartine.
      CFP #C3. (5:30).

205. DEERING, RICHARD (c. 1580-1630). Gaudent in
      caelis, ed. Bruno Turner. TT. org. Lat. Text:
      Magnificat, antiphon from 2nd vespers, Common of
      two or more Martyrs. ACM #437.

206. DEERING. O bone Jesu, ed. Turner. TT. org.
      Lat. Text: trad. sacred. AMP #A437.

207. DEERING. Quem irdistis pastores, ed. Biester.
      Lat. Eng. TTBB. LGGS #51758.

208. de GIARDINI, FELICE (1716-1796). Let's Drink
      (Beviamo), ed. William Tortolano. TTB. Unac.
      It. MF #1057.

209. de HOLLAND, JEAN (16c.). That Nightingale at
      Rest in Singing (Le Rossignol dans son Nid chante),
      ed. Don Malin. TTBB. Unac. Eng. Text: Malin.
      BEL #OCT 2330.

210. DELANEY, ROBERT (1903-1956). Blow, Blow, Thou
      Winter Wind. TTBB. pf. Eng. Text: Shakes-
      peare: As You Like It. Act II, sc. 7. ECS #2103.

211. DELANEY. Full Fathom Five Thy Father Lies.
      TTBB. pf. Eng. Text: Shakespeare: Tempest,
      Act II; sc. 2 ECS #2102.

212. DEL ENCINA, JUAN (1468-1529). Let Us Eat Drink
      and Be Merry (Oy Comamos y Bebamos), ed. Don
      Malin. TTBB. Unac. Sp. Eng. BEL #OCT 2328.
      (1:25).

213. DELIUS, FREDERICK (1862-1934). Wanderer's Song.
      TTBB (some div. in all parts). pf. Eng. Ger.
      Text: R. S. Hoffman. Eng. Arthur Symons. BH
      #1634.

214. DELLO JOIO, NORMAN (1913-). O Sing Unto the
      Lord. TBB. org. Eng. Text: Ps. 98. CF
      #7138. (4:00). Composed 1959.

215. DE SERMISY, CLAUDIN (1490-1562). Ceulx de Pi-
      cardie (Picardy has Burghers), ed. Isabelle Caz-
      eaux. TTBB. Unac. Fr. Text: unknown. Eng.
      vers. Cazeaux. ALB #133-5. (0:30).

216. DE SERMISY. Lux aeterna (Etermal Light), ed.
      H. T. Luce. TTBB. Unac. Eng. Text: Requiem
      Mass. BR #NC2.

217. DES PREZ, JOSQUIN (1450-1521). (Also known as
      des Pres). Agnus Dei from Missa de Beata Vir-
      gine, ed. Paul Boepple. TB. Unac. MP #25.
      (1:10).

218. DES PREZ. Missa Mater Patris, ed. Elliot Forbes.
      TTBB. Unac. Lat. (parody Mass based on Brumel
      motif of the same name). GS #2642. (Gloria is
      6:00).

219. DES PREZ. Pleni sunt coeli from Missa Pange Lin-
      gua, ed. Boepple. TB. Unac. Lat. MP #25.

220. DES PREZ. Tu pauperum refugium, arr. WRS.
      TTBB. Unac. Lat unknown. ECS #82.

221. DIAMOND, DAVID (1915-). Let Us All Take to
      Singing. TTBB. Unac. Eng. Text: Herman Mel-
      ville. SOU #ME-1003.

222. DIAMOND. The Martyr. TTBB. Unac. Eng. Text:
      Melville. SOU #ME1004. (10:00).

223. DIEMER, EMMA LOU (1927-). O Come Let Us
      Sing Unto the Lord. TTBB. pf/org. Originally
      for SATB, but arranged for male voices by the
      composer. Eng. Text: CF.

224. DIEMER. Three Poems. TTBB. FLAM #C5015.

225. DIRKSEN, RICHARD (1921-). Three Songs of
      Prayer and Praise. TBB (SSA). SP.

226. DISTLER, HUGO (1908-1942). Abendlied eines Reisen-
      den (Evening Song of a Traveller), ed. C. G.
      Ticher. TTBB. Unac. Ger. Eng. EAM #B238.

227. DISTLER. Mörike--Chorliederbuch, Teil III (Vol.
      III), op. 19. 2-5 men's voices. Unac. Ger. BAR-
      EN #BA 1518. Titles: Agnes; An Philomele; Der
      Gartner; Der Liebhaber and die Heisse Quelle; Der
      Tambour Frage und Antwort; Jagerlied; Jung Volk-
      er (Gesang der Rauber); Jung Volkers Lied; Lamm-
      wirts Klagelied; Lied eines Verliebten; Verborgen-
      heit. The first vol. is for SATB. The second
      for SSAA. Some of the 12 pieces in Vol. 3 are
      available separately. Of particular interest are
      Tambour, Jagerlied, An Philomele, Lied eines
      Verliebten.

228. DONATI, BALDASSARE (-1603). Non vos relin-
      quam orphanos, ed. Jerome Roche. Lat. TTB.
      keyboard. OX.

229. DONATO, ANTHONY (1909-). Homesick Blues.
      TTBB. Unac. Text: Langston Hughes, from the
      Dream Keeper. MMC #320.

230. DONIZETTI, GAETANO (1797-1848). La Figlia del
      Regimento: The Soldier's Chorus. (Act 1). adap.
      S. Northcote. TTBB. Eng. Text: Ed. Miller.
      RIC #LD 472. (1:45). Also NOV #OP. CH26
      and 27.

231. DONIZETTI. Lucia di Lamermoor: Percorriamo le
      spiagge vicine. Act 1, sc. 1. Based on the Wal-

ter Scott novel. TTB. T. solo. pf. Text:
Salvatore Cammarano. GS. (3:00).

232. DONOVAN, RICHARD (1891-1970). Fantasy on American Folk Ballads. TTBB. pf. 4 hands or 2 pi-
anos T. or S. solos. Eng. Texts: American Folk.
(1) I Pitch my Tent on This Campground. (2) Farewell, My Friends. (3) Old Bangum. (4) Ballad of
Courtship from Danville, Vermont. (5) Reuben Ran-
zo. JF #7737 (13:00). Composed 1940.

233. DONOVAN. Good Ale. TTBB. Unac. Eng. Text:
John Still. CP #CM 6242. (3:30).

234. DONOVAN. I Will Sing Unto the Lord. TTBB. Bar.
solo. Eng. Text: adapted from Scripture. AUG.
(8:30). Composed 1959.

235. DONOVAN. Mass (1955). For Unison Voices (or
opt. 2 and 3 pts.). Org. 3 Tr. Timp. ACA.
(12:00).

236. DUFAY, GUILLAUME (c. 1400-1474). Gloria ad
modum tubae (canon), ed. William Tortolano. 2
parts (TB or SA). org/2 tr. Lat. GIA #G2150.
Also in Renaissance to Baroque, vol. 1, ed. Leh-
mann Engel.

237. DUFAY. Gloria orbis factor, ed. Tortolano. Unis.
voices. org/2 va/vln. vc. Lat. GIA #G2149.

238. DUFAY. Kyrie dominicale, ed. Tortolano. Unis.
voices. org/vln. va./vln. vc. Lat. GIA #G2148.

239. DUFAY. Kyrie orbis factor, ed. Tortolano. Unis.
voices, org/2 va/vn. vc. Lat. GIA #G2148.

240. DUFAY. Magnificat in the Eighth Mode, ed. Boepple.
TB (and instruments). Lat. Text: Luke 1:46-56.
MMC #MC 29. (5:00).

241. DUNSTABLE, JOHN (1370-1453). Sancta Maria, ed.
Bernard Rose. TBB. Unac. Lat. Text: Unknown.
SB #5283.

242. DURUFLE, MAURICE (1902-). Messe cum Jubilo.
Unis. B. solo. org. (and orch.). Lat. Text:
Mass. DUR.

243. DVORAK, ANTONIN (1841-1904). Five Choruses, op.
27: (1) Village Gossip. (2) Dwellers by the Sea.
(3) The Promise of Love. (4) The Lost Lamb.
(5) The Sparrows Party. All TTBB. Unac. Eng.
Texts by Ross Newmarch, based on traditional
texts. CHES #JWC 5702, 3, 4, 5, 6.

244. DVORAK. Gram (Grief) from 3 slovak Men's Songs,
op. 43, no. 1, ed. Woodworth. TTBB. pf. 4
hands. Eng. Text: Ger. Th. Cürsch-Bühren.
GS #9813.

245. DVORAK. Mägdlein im Walde (Maiden in the World)
from 3 Slovak Men's Songs, op. 43, no. 3, ed.
Woodworth. TTBB. pf. 4 hands. Eng. Text:
Ger. Cürsch-Bühren. GS #9812. Only 2 songs
from op. 43 are published.

246. DVORAK. Stabat Mater, op. 58: Fac me vere tecum
flere. Scene 6. TTBB. T. solo. orch. reduced
for pf. Lat. KAL #6162. Also NOV. Eng.; GS
4572.

247. EDWARDS, SHERMAN. 1776 (A Musical): For God's
Sake, Sit Down John. TTBB. Unac.

248. ELGAR, SIR EDWARD (1857-1934). Five Part Songs
from the Greek Anthology, op. 45. (1) Yea, Cast
Me From the Heights of the Mountain. Text: Anon.
Greek. Eng. Trans. Alma Strettel. (2) Whether I
Find Thee. Text: Anon. Greek. Eng. Trans. An-
drew Lang. (3) After Many a Dusty Mile. Text:
Anon. Greek. Eng. Trans. Edmond Gosse. (4)
It's Oh! To Be a Wild Wind. Text: Anon. Greek.
Eng. trans. W. M. Hardinge. (5) Feasting I Watch.
Marcus Argentarius. Eng. trans. Richard Garnett.
All TTBB. Unac. Ger. trans. Julius Buths. NOV.

249. ELGAR. The Reveille. TTBB. Unac. Eng. Text:
Bret Harte. NOV #449.

250. ELGAR. Zut! Zut! Zut! (Remember). TTBB. Unac. Eng. Text: Richard Mardon. NOV #591.

251. ENGLISH, ANON. Alleluia Psallat (13c.), ed. Stevens. TTT (SSS). Unac. Lat. NOV #MT 1463.

252. ENGLISH. Angelus ad Virginem, ed. and arr. Denis

Stevens. TTB (SSA). Lat. MP #909. "He made
a nightes melodye so swetely, that as the chambre
song, and angelus ad Virginem he sang," from
"The Miller's Tale," Canterbury Tales, Chaucer.

253. ENGLISH, ANON, 16C. O bone Jesu, ed. H. B.
Collins. TTBB. Unac. CHES.

254. ENGLISH, ANON. Sanctus and Benedictus (ca. 1310).
A. T. solos. with men's choir, ed. Stevens. Lat.
BR. Taken from the Treasury of English Music.

255. ENGLISH, ANON. Three Early Medieval Settings:
(1) Alleluia Psallat (ca. 1290). 3T, soli and
chorus. (2) Sanctus and Benedictus (ca. 1375).
A and 2T solos, chorus. (3) Kyrie (Orbis Factor).
Ca. 1300. 2A and T solos, chorus of unison men.
Trans. and ed. Denis Stevens. Lat. Taken from
the Treasury of English Music. BB.

256. ESTE, MICHAEL (1580-1648). How Merrily We Live,
ed. H. Clough-Leighter. TTB. Unac. Eng. Text:
Anon. ECS #756. (2:00).

257. EVETT, ROBERT (1922-). The Last Supper.
TTBB. TBB solos. fl. ob. harpsichord. Eng.
ACA.

258. FELCIANO, RICHARD (1930-). Benedictio Nuptialis
(Marriage Blessing). Unis. Org. ECS #2518.

259. FELCIANO. Double Alleluia. Alleluia-Send Forth
Thy Spirit. Ps. 103:30. Alleluia--Come, Holy
Spirit. Sequence--Come Thou Holy Spirit. Assigned
to Stephen Langton. Unis. org. electronic tape
(available from the publishers). Eng. WL #EEMP-
532-1. (3:30).

260. FELCIANO. Give Thanks Unto the Lord. Unis. org.
Eng. ECS.

261. FELCIANO. Songs for Darkness and Light. TBB
(SSA). Unac. Eng. in 4 mvt. (1) I Will Sing to
the Lord. (2) My Friend Had a Vineyard. (3)
Give Ear, O Heavens. (4) As the Hind Longs for
the Running Water. ECS #2805.

262. FELCIANO. Two Hymns to Howl By. 4 ev. Unac.
      Eng. Text: Allen Ginsberg. ECS #2239.

263. FINE, IRVING (1914-1962). Pianola d'Amore from
      The Choral New Yorker. Modern Madrigal for
      TBB. pf. Eng. Text: David McCord. CF.

264. FINZI, GERALD (1901-1956). Thou Dids't Delight
      My Eyes. TBB. Text: Robert Bridges. BH
      #5356.

265. FLOYD, CARLISLE (1926-). Death Comes Knocking.
      TTBB. pf. Eng. Text: Joseph Auslander. BH
      #5368. Composed 1961.

266. FOREST, JOHN. Little Lamb, Who Made Thee.
      TTBB. Unac. Eng. Text: William Blake, from
      Songs of Innocence. SP C5063. (2:45).

267. FORTNER, WOLFGANG (1907-). Die Entschlafen
      "Eine Verganglichen Tag." TTBB. Unac. Ger.
      SCH #C. 33. 746. Composed 1933. Text: Höl-
      derlin.

268. FRACKENPOHL, ARTHUR (1924-). Essays on
      Women. TTBB. pf. Eng. Text: Ogden Nash.
      CP 04698. In 7 mvts: (1) Pants and Paint. (2)
      The Feminine Approach to Feminine Fashions.
      (3) To My Valentine. (4) Lady Limericks. (5)
      The Ladies of the Garden Club. (6) Women Sitting
      Firmly on Their Coats. (7) A Nice Girl with a
      Naughty Word. CF #04698.

269. FRACKENPOHL. Lovers Love the Spring (It Was a
      Lover and His Lass). TBB. pf. (opt. Guitar,
      drums, stb.). Eng. Text: Shakespeare: As You
      Like It. Act. V, Sc. 3. EBM #110. (2:00).

270. FRACKENPOHL. Shepherds, Rejoice. TTBB. T.
      or B. solo. Brass Choir: 3 hns. F, 2 Tromb.
      Bar. tuba. Text: The Social Harp, Philadelphia,
      1868. RK. (4:00).

271. FRACKENPOHL. Three Limericks in Canon Form.
      (1) A Diner at Crewe. (2) A Boy of Bagdad. (3)
      A Fellow of Perth. TBB. pf. Eng. Text: Tra-
      ditional. EBM #114. (1:50; 1:30; 0:50).

272. FRANCK, CESAR (1822-1890). Panis Angelicus, ed.
     Arthur Ryder. TTBB. T. solo. Org. Eng. Text:
     Ryder. BMC #447.

273. FRANCO, JOHAN (1908-). Ode. TTBB and sym-
     phonic band. Text: Eloise Franco. ACA.

274. FRANCO. Psalm and Alleluia. TBB. Unac. ACA.

275. FRIDERICI, DANIEL (1584-1638). Within Our Hearts
     We Cherish (Wir Lieben sehr ihm Herzen), ed.
     Don Malin. Ger. Eng. Text: Malin. BEL #Oct.
     2332.

276. FRIML, RUDOLF (1879-1972). Song of the Vagabonds
     from the Vagabond King, ed. Simeone. TTBB.
     pf. Eng. Text: Brian Hooker. SP #C140.

277. FROMM, HERBERT (1905-). Stephano's Song from
     the Tempest, Act II, sc. 2. TTBB. Unac. Eng.
     Text: Shakespeare. ECS #2198.

278. GABRIELI, GIOVANNI (1557-1612). Surrexit Christus,
     ed. Hewitt Pantaleoni. TTB. org. or pf. Text:
     Lat. paraphrase of Luke 24:34. Eng. Pantaleoni.
     CON #97-6370.

279. GABURO, KENNETH (1926-). Mass for Tenors and
     Basses. TB. WL.

280. GERICKE, WILHELM (1845-1925). Chorus of Homage.
     TTBB. pf. Eng. Text: Eng. vers. Louis C. El-
     son. BMC #859.

281. GERICKE. The Autumn Sea, op. 8, no. 3. TTBB.
     Unac. Text: Eng. vers. Dr. Theodore Baker.
     BMC #134.

282. GERMAN, EDWARD (1862-1936). O Peaceful Night.
     TTBB. Unac. Eng. Text: W. Herbert Scott.
     NOV #497.

283. GERSHEFSKI, EDWIN (1909-). The Lord's Con-
     troversy with His People. TTBB. T. solo. Unac.
     Eng. ACA.

284. GIBBONS, ORLANDO (1583-1625). O Lord, Increase

My Faith, arr. Howard Hinners. TTBB. Unac.
Eng. Text: Unknown. GR #671.

285. GILL, MILTON (1932-1968). O Lord, Rebuke Me
Not. TTBB. Unac. Eng. Text: Ps. 6. SMC.

286. GINASTERA, ALBERTO (1916-). Arriero, Canta!
(Sing Muleteer). TTBB. Unac. Eng. Sp. Text:
Felix Errico. Eng. Lorraine Finley. BMC #2968.

287. GOLD. Now You Are Departed from Songs on American Indian Lyrics. TTBB. Unac. Fr. hn. obbli-
gato. LGGS #565.

288. GOULD, MORTON (1933-). Prayer of Micah (Who
Is a God Like unto Thee). TTBB. pf/org. Eng.
AMHERST PRESS.

289. GOOSEN, FREDERIC (1927-). Death, Be Not Proud.
TTBB. Unac. Eng. SOU PIC 2263-10.

290. GOUNOD, CHARLES (1818-1893). There are several
choruses by Gounod for men's voices that are well
worth looking at: (1) Beau Voyageur, TTBB. Unac. Fr. LEM. (2) Funeral March of a Marionette.
TTBB. ENOCH. (3) La Chasse. TTBB. CHOU.
(4) Melodrame (from Ulysse), men's chorus. CHOU.
La Chasse available from NOV #Orph. 23.

291. GOUNOD. Sicut cervus (As Parts the Heart). TTBB.
Unac. Lat. Text: GS #550.

292. GOUNOD. Soldier's Chorus, from Faust. TTBB.
pf. Eng. Text: Barbier and Carré. GS #4283.
Also TP #312-20196. (4:45).

293. GREENE, MAURICE (1695-1755). Loudly Shout His
Praise. TBB. pf. Eng. CON.

294. GRETCHANINOFF, ALEXANDER (1864-1956). Glory
to God. TTBB. Unac. Eng. Text: Mass Text.
EBM #53. (3:15).

295. GRETCHANINOFF. O God, Hear My Prayer. TTBB.
Eng. Unac. FMC #1291.

296. GRETCHANINOFF. Nunc dimittis. TTTTBBBB. Unac.
FMC #825.

297. GRETCHANINOFF.   The Cherubic Hymn, arr. by the
      composer. TTBB. Unac. Eng. Text: Russian
      Liturgy of St. John Chrysostum.   JF #8667.

298. GRIEG, EDVARD (1843-1907).   Landerkennung (Recog-
      nition of the Land), op. 31.   TTBB.   pf. Bar.
      solo. Eng. Fr. Ger. Norw. Text: Björnstjerne
      Björnson.   CFP #2805.   (7:00).   Also GS #1013.
      Eng. Ger.

299. GRIEG.   Zwei Gesänge aus Sigurd Jorsalfar, op. 22.
      TTBB. Bar. solo. pf. Ger. Text: Björnson.
      CFP #2660.

300. GRIEG.   Zwölf Chöre nach Norwegischen Wersen
      (Album for Male Voices, op. 30. 8 choruses based
      on Norwegian Folk, including Grieg's favorite: The
      Great White Host).   TTBB. Bar. solo. Unac.
      Text: Eng. trans. Percy Grainger.   CFP #2492.
      (1) I Laid Me Down to Slumber. (2) Children's
      Song. (3) Little Thora. (4) Kusslin's Haling.
      (5) There Is No Folly Half So Great. (6) When
      I Take a Stroll. (7) The Great White Host. (8)
      Rötsans-Kunt.

301. GUMPELTZHAIMER, ADAM (1559-1625).   Coenam
      cum discipulis, ed. Robert Shaw. TTBB. Unac.
      Lat. Ger. Eng. GS #9961.

302. HABA, ALOIS (1898-1972).   Chorsuite, op. 13.   In
      quarter tones. Male, female or mixed voices.
      Unac. UN.

303. HADLEY, HENRY (1871-1937).   Night. TTBB. Unac.
      Eng. Text: Washburn Harding. ROW #330. (1:00).

304. HAMMERSCHMIDT, ANDREAS (1612-1675).   Lobet
      den Herren, meine seele. TT(SS). pf. HVS
      #HE 5. 174.

305. HAMMERSCHMIDT.   Verleeh uns Frieden Gnadiglich.
      TT(SS). pf. HVS #HE 5, 175.

      HANDL, JACOB (1550-1592).   (Also known as Jacobus
      Gallus). 39 original works for men's voices can
      be found in the musicological collection, Denkmäler,
      BHL. These are in Latin in various vocal ranges

from TTTT to TTBBTTBB. Originally one or
more tenor parts would have been for Alto (male).

306. HANDL. Confirma hoc Deus (Confirm in Us, O
      Lord), ed. Mason Martens. TTBB. Unac. Lat.
      Eng. Text: Based on Ps. 67:29, 30, by Martens.
      CON #498-1655. Also AB.

307. HANDL. O magnum mysterium, arr. Howard Mc-
      Kinney. TTBB, TTBB. Unac. Lat. Text: Re-
      sponsory, Matins, Christmas; Paraphrase of Luke
      2:10-13. JF #7539. Also, AB. (2:30).

308. HANDL. Regnum mundi from Opus Musicum Harmon-
      iarum, ed. Paul Boepple. TTBB. Unac. Lat.
      Text: Non-Biblical, Roman Breviary. MMC
      Also. AB. (1:00).

309. HANDL. Repleti sunt omnes, ed. Boepple. TTBB-
      TTBB (SSAA-SSAA). Unac. Lat. Text: Acts 2:4,
      11. MMC #MC31. Also AB. (1:30).

310. HANDL. Resonet in laudibus (Let the Voice of Praise
      Resound), ed. Bernard Rainbow. NOV #MV147.

311. HANDL. Trahe me post te, ed. Boepple. TTBBB.
      Unac. Lat Text: Songs of Solomon 1:3.2. MMC
      #MC32. (1:00).

312. HANNAY, ROGER (1930-). Christmas Tide. GAL
      #1.2341.1.

313. HANSON, HOWARD (1896-). Song of Democracy,
      op. 44. TTBB. Eng. Text: Walt Whitman. Orch.
      score reduced for pf. by Maurice Ford. CF.
      (12:00). Commissioned by the National Educational
      Assn. for its 100th anniversary and the National
      Music Educators Conference for its 50th anniver-
      sary. (12:00).

314. HARRIS, ROY (1898-1979). Freedom's Land. TTBB.
      Unac. Eng. Text: Archibald MacLeish. BEL
      #64425.

315. HARRIS. Mass for Male Voices and Organ. Lat.
      TTBB. CF (on rental only). (30:00).

316. HARRIS. The Working Man's Pride; Folk Fantasy

for Festivals. TTBB, Bass-Bar. solo. speaker.
Eng. Texts: American Folk. AMP.

317. HARRISON, LOU (1919-). A Joyous Procession
and a Solemn Procession. H and L Voices. 2
tromb. Also in (1) 4 tamborines and gong. (2)
8 handbells (4 players), large bass drum. Text:
wordless. CFP #6534. (6:00). Written in 1962
for the Nuns of Immaculate Heart College, Los
Angeles.

318. HARRISON. Mass for Male and Female Voices (Also known as St. Anthony Mass). All in unis. tr.
harp and str. Lat. (possible to do with men only).
ACA. (28:00).

319. HASSLER, HANS LEO (1564-1612). Cantate Domino,
arr. Archibald T. Davison. TTBB. Unac. Lat.
Text: Ps. 96:1-3. ECS #68. (2:00). Also CON
#98-341; BOURNE, #H1486; ECS #2194, ed. Beve-
ridge. (2:00).

320. HASSLER. Domine Deus, ed. Swing. TTBB. Unac.
Lat. Eng. Text: Ps. 96:1-3; 11-13. CON #98-
1341.

321. HASSLER. Gratias agimus tibi, ed. Peter Gram
Swing. TTBB. Unac. Lat. Eng. Text: Mass
Text. CON #98-1342. (out of print).

322. HASSLER. Laetentur coeli, ed. Swing. TTBB. Unac. Lat. Eng. Ps. 95:11-13 (4 original male motets
by Hassler according to Swing: Laetentur caeli;
Cantate Domino; Domine Deus; Gratias agimus tibi).
CON #98-1339. Also NOV #136, ed. B. Rainbow.

323. HASSLER. God Now Dwells Among Us (Verbum caro
factum est), ed. Roger Wilhelm. TBB. pf. or.
org. Lat. Eng. Text: Unknown. MF. (2:00).

324. HASTINGS, ROSS (1915-). To Electra. TTBB.
pf. Eng. Text: Robert Herrick. CAN #6802.

325. HAUSSMANN, VALENTIN (16-17C.). With Sighing
and Lament (Mit Seufzen und mit Klag), ed. Don
Malin. TTBB. Unac. Ger. Eng. Text: Malin.
BEL #OLT 2331. (5:00).

326. HAYDN, FRANZ JOSEPH (1732-1809). Dreistimmige
Gesänge (Three-Part-Songs). TTBB. pf. Ger. (1)
An die Frauen. Text: Second Ode of Anacreon,
Trans. G. A. Bürger. (2) Daphnes einziger Fehler.
Text: Anon. CFP #4936. Also, An die Frauen,
ed. J. C. De Witt, TP & MC 276.

327. HAYDN. Maiden Fair, O Deign to Tell. Eng. vers.
Thomas Oliphant. TTB. pf. Text: Oliphant.
GR #527.

328. HEATH, FENNO (1926-). Death Be Not Proud.
TTBB. Unac. Eng. Text: John Donne. GS
#11975. Composed for The Yale Glee Club Cen-
tennial, 1960-1961.

329. HEILLER, ANTON (1923-1979). Exsurge Domine
(from the Introit, Sexagesima Sunday). TTTBBB.
Lat. UE #11795. (6:30). Composed 1947.

330. HENRY VIII, KING (1491-1547). Quam pulchra es,
ed. Thurston Dart. TTB. Unac. Lat. Text: Solomon 7:6, 7, 5, 4, 11, 12. The only surviving
piece of Latin music by this king. SB #5565.

331. HENSCHEL, GEORG (1850-1934). Morning Hymn,
op. 46, no. 4. TTBB. pf. Ger. Text: Robert
Reinick, Eng. Trans. Dirk van der Stucken. CF
#CM 2126. (2:00). Also BMC #2133. Henschel
was a singer and the first conductor of the Boston
Symphony.

332. HINDEMITH, PAUL (1895-1963). Der Tod. Unac.
Ger. Text: Friedrich Hölderlin. SCH #33527.

333. HINDEMITH. Du muss die Alles geben from Drei
Männerchöre. (1930). Unac. Ger. Text: Gottfried
Benn. SCH #32784.

334. HINDEMITH. Eine lichte Mitternacht from Zwei Männerchöre. (1929). TTBB. Unac. Text: Walt Whitman. Ger. Trans. Johannes Schlaf. SCH #32548.

335. HINDEMITH. Erster Schnee. TTBB. Unac. Ger.
Text: Gottfried Keller. SCH #37483.

336. HINDEMITH. Fürst Kraft from Drei Männerchöre,

1930. TTBB. Unac. Ger. Text: Gottfried Benn.
SCH #32783.

337. HINDEMITH. Galgenritt (The Demon of the Gibbet).
TBB. Eng. Ger. Text: Fitz-James O'Brien. SCH
#37535.

338. HINDEMITH. Über das Frůjahr from Zwei Männerchöre, 1929. TTBB. Unac. Ger. Text: Bertolt
Brecht. SCH #32545.

339. HINDEMITH. Variationen über ein altes Tanzlied
(Das jung auch das alte). TTBB. Unac. Ger.
Text: Old German. SCH #37584.

340. HINDEMITH. Vision des Mannes from Drei Männerchöre, 1930. TTBB. Unac. Ger. Text: Gottfried
Benn. SCH #32785.

341. HODDINOTT, ALUN (1929-). Four Welsh Songs.
TTBB. pf. orch: 2222/4230/timp. hp/str. (1)
The Yellow Sheepskin. (2) The Poet's Dream.
(3) Fair Lisa. (4) The Lazy Wife. Eng. Text:
Rhiannon Huddinott (from the Welsh). Also avail-
able in Unis. settings. OX. (10:00).

342. HOLLER, KARL (1907-). Media Vita, op. 8 (motet). Men's chorus. Unac. Lat. Leuck, c/o AMP.

343. HOLST, GUSTAV (1864-1934). Choral Hymns from
the Rig Veda (Fourth Group), op. 26. TTBB.
orch. reduction for pf. Eng. (1) Hymn to Agni
(the sacrificial fire). (2) Hymn to Soma (Soma is
the juice of an herb used in sacrifice). (3) Hymn
to Manas (an invocation to the Manas or spirit of
a dying man). (4) Hymn to Indra (Indra is the God
of Heaven, storm, and battle). GR #291, 292, 294.
Orch: 2 tr. 2 hns, 3 tromb. hp/pf, str.

344. HOLST. Dirge for Two Veterans. TTBB. pf. or
2 tr. B-flat, 2 tromb. (or tromb. and tuba), side
drum, bass drum. Text: Walt Whitman. GS
#8323. (instrumental parts on rental).

345. HOLST. I Vow Thee My Country. (Melody taken
from Jupitor, no. 4 of the Planets). Unis. pf.
Eng. Text: Sir C. S. Rice. GS #11334.

346. HOLST. Six Choruses for Male Voices, op. 53.
      (1) Good Friday. TTBB. pf/org-str. Eng. Text:
      Helen Waddell, from the Lat. of Peter Abelard.
      BH #5923. Dedicated to Westminster Abbey Choir.
      (2) Intercession. TTBB. pf/org/str. Eng. Text:
      Waddell. from the Lat. of Sedulius Scottus. BH
      #5924. Dedicated to the Holme Valley Choir. (3)
      How Mighty are the Sabbaths. TTBB. pf/org/str.
      Eng. Text: Waddell, from the Lat. of Abelard.
      BH #5925. Dedicated to the Harvard Glee Club.
      There is an ad lib. chorus for treble voices in
      unis. (4) A Love Song (Canon). TTBB. pf. str.
      Eng. Text: Waddell from the Lat. MSS of Bene-
      dictbeuren. BH #5924. (5) Drinking Song. TTBB.
      pf/str. Eng. Text: BH #5927. Dedicated to the
      Winnipeg Male Voice Choir. (6) Before Sleep. TB
      (Canon). org/pf/str. Eng. Text: Waddell, from
      the Lat. of Prudentius. BH #5928. Dedicated to
      the Harvard Glee Club. (5:30 for How Mighty).

347. HOLST. Song of the Lumberman. 2 pts. pf. Eng.
      Text: John G. Whittier. OX.

348. HOLST. Song of the Shipbuilders. 2 ev. Eng. Text:
      Whittier. OX.

349. HOLST. Traditional Folk Songs. TTBB. Unac.
      Eng. (1) I Love My Love. (2) I Sowed the Seeds.
      (3) In the Bleak Mid Winter. (4) Lullay My Liking.
      (5) Matthew, Mark, Luke, and John. (6) The Song
      of the Blacksmith. (7) Swansee Town. (8) Wassail
      Song. GS.

350. HONEGGER, ARTHUR (1892-1955). King David: Song
      of the Prophets. TB. pf. Fr. Text: René Mor-
      ax. Eng. Edward Agate. FF. (1:15). Composed
      1921.

351. HOVHANESS, ALAN (1911-). Protest and Prayer,
      op. 41. TTBB. T. solo. org. Eng. Text: Hov-
      haness. CFP #66198. (10:00). Composed 1969.

352. HOVHANESS. To the God Who Is in the Fire, op.
      146. TTBB. 6 perc. players (Marimba I, Marim-
      ba II, A & E pedal timp B. Drum, Tam-Tam). T.
      solo, Eng. Text: Sh'vet Upanished II, 17. CFP
      #6509A. (6:00). Composed 1967.

353. HUSTAD, JEAN. A New Song. TTBB. Unac. Eng.
      Text: Ps. 96, HOPE #9003.

354. IBERT, JACQUES (1890-1962). Deux Chants de Car-
      naval. 3 ev. Unac. Fr. Text: Machiavelli. HEU.

355. IMBRIE, ANDREW (1921-). Psalm 42. TBB. org.
      Eng. Text: Ps. 42:1, 2, 5, 7, 8, 11. CFP #6888.
      (6:00). Commissioned by Colgate Univ. 1965.

356. ISAAK, HEINRICH (1450-1517). Innsbruck, ich muss
      dich lassen.

357. IVES, CHARLES (1874-1954). December. Men unis.
      Unac, or woodwind and brass. Eng. Text: Folgore
      da San Geminiano-Rossetti (Ives?). PEER #812-2.
      (2:00). Composed 1912-13.

358. IVES. For You and Me, ed. Clifford Richter. TTBB.
      Unac. Eng. Text: Unknown. JB #124. (1:00).

359. IVES. Lincoln the Great Commoner: Let There Be
      Light. TTBB. Unac. Eng. Text: John Ellerton.
      "The voices can be mixed or women's or men's
      chorus," Ives. pf/orch: 2222/0242/timp. pf/str.
      Eng. Text: Edwin Markham. Composed in 1912.
      TP. Also, SOU #ME1019. (5:00).

360. IVES. Serenity. Unis. pf. Eng. Text: John G.
      Whittier. AMP #A377.

361. IVES. They Are There (War Song). Unis. but not
      necessarily all male voices. pf. Eng. Text: Ives.
      PEER #607-6, c/o SOU. (3:00).

362. JAMES, PHILIP (1890-?). General William Booth
      Enters Heaven (Salvation Army Founder). TTBB.
      tr. C. tromb. perc. (1 player): tam-tam, B. drum.
      tamb. 2 pianos (2nd interchangeable with organ).
      Eng. Text: Nicholas Vachel Lindsay. WIT. (10:00).

363. JANACEK, LEOS (1854-1928). Cantata: Na soláni
      carták. TTBB, T solo. Orch: 2322/4000/timp,
      perc, hp/org/str. Text: Maximillian Kunert.
      Czech, Ger. Eng. BH. (6:30).

364. JANACEK. Constitues. TTBB. org. UW #14982.

Written for the offertory Constitues for a High
Mass in the Cathedral at Brno. Composed in
1903.

365. JANACEK. Tři Můzské Sbory (Three Male Choruses).
Ger. There is a recording of Janacek's music:
Famous Male Choruses by the Moravian Teachers'
Choir on the Supraphon label #H-71288.

366. KAHN, ERICH ITOR (1905-1956). Rhapsodie Hassidique. TTBB. Unac. (if the intonation problems
are extreme, the composer has provided a wind
instrumentation: E. Hn. cl. in A, Bcl. bn. 2 hns.
F, tromb. org.). Heb. Text: Traditional Hassidic
(Hebrew phonetics provided). ACA.

367. KASLTE, LEONARD (1929-). Three Whale Songs:
Moby Dick. TTBB. Unac. T. solo. Eng. Text:
unknown. RIC #NY2246.

368. KAY, ULYSSES (1917-). Come Away, Come Away,
Death. TBB. Unac. Eng. Text: Shakespeare,
Twelfth Night. SOU #ME1014. (3:00). Composed
1943.

369. KAY. Triple Set. (1) Ode to the Cuckoo (TB). (2)
Had I a Heart (TB). (3) A Toast (TBB). Unac.
Eng. Texts: (1) Michael Bruce. (2) Richard Brins-
ley Sheridan. (3) Sheridan. MCA #19519-125;
19543-125.

370. KAY. Triumvirate: (1) Music. (2) The Children's
Hour. (3) The Night Watch. TTBB. Unac. Eng.
Texts: (1) Ralph Waldo Emerson. (2) Henry Wads-
worth Longfellow. (3) Herman Melville. Commissioned for the DePaur Infantry Chorus, 1954.

371. KEENAN, KENT (1913-). The Unknown Warrior
Speaks. TTBB. Unac. Eng. Text: Margery
Smith (from Poems of This War, pub. Cambridge).
GR #5.

372. KELLEY, ROBERT (1916-). The Torment of Job,
op. 36. Men's chorus. 3 tr. 3 tbn/pf. perc. narrator. ACA.

373. KENNEDY, JOHN DRODBIN (1934-). Down by The

Salley Gardens. TTB. pf. Eng. Text: W. B.
Yeats. BH #5840.

374.   KENNEDY. Little Lamb, Who Made Thee. TB.
       pf. Eng. Text: William Blake. BH #5654.

375.   KINDERMANN, Johann (1616-1655). Creator Spirit,
       by Whose Aid, ed. Fritz Oberdoeffer. TB. 2
       vln. cont. Eng. Text: attr. Rhabanus Maurus,
       trans. John Dryden. CON #98-1482. (3:00).

376.   KODALY, ZOLTAN (1882-1967). Several male Kodá-
       ly choruses are on the recording "Songs for Tip-
       plers, Monks and Patriots." Whikehart Chorale.
       Lyrichord #LL7208. The Bachelor. TBB. Unac.
       Text: Folk Song from Szekelg. Eng. vers. Nancy
       Bush. BH #1893. Composed 1934.

377.   KODALY. Drinking Song. TTBB. Unac. Eng. Text:
       orig. Hung. Ferenc Kilcsey. Eng. trans. Matyas
       Seiber, Leo Black. TP #7445A. (6:00). Com-
       posed 1913.

378.   KODALY. Evening Song. TBB. Unac. Text: Eng.
       trans. Geoffrey Russell-Smith. BH #5798.

379.   KODALY. God's Mercy (Isten Csodája). TBB. Un-
       ac. Hung. Text: Sàndor Petofi. Eng. Text: Geof-
       frey Russell-Smith. BH #5877.

380.   KODALY. The Peacocks (Husat). TBB. Unac. Eng.
       trans. Nancy Bush. BH #1894. (3:00). Composed 1951.

381.   KODALY. The Ruins. TBB. Unac. Text: Eng.
       vers. Elizabeth M. Lockwood. UN #312-405595.
       (3:00). Also, with pf, perc. Composed 1938.

382.   KODALY. Soldier's Song. TBB. tr. snare drum.
       Text: Eng. vers. Nancy Bush. BH #1892. (3:30).
       Composed 1934.

383.   KODALY. Songs from Karad. TBB. Unac. Eng.
       trans. Nancy Bush. BH #1894. (5:00). Composed
       1951.

384.   KODALY. Tavern Song. TTBB. Unac. Eng. Text:
       Anon. 17th Century. Eng. trans. Matyas Seiber,
       Leo Black. TP #7445B. (2:15). Composed 1917.

385. KOHN, KARL (1926-   ). A Latin Fable. Men's
    Chorus. Unac. (5:00).

386. KOHN. Three Goliard Songs: (1) Exit diluculo.
    (2) Stetit puella. (3) Tempus hoc letitie. TBB.
    Unac. Lat. Text: Medieval Latin Goliard Songs.
    CF #07432. (2:40; 1:25; 1:30).

387. KOHS, ELLIS (1916-   ). The Automatic Pistol (Sol-
    dier's Handbook). TB. Unac. ACA.

388. KOHS. Three Medieval Latin Student Songs. Trans.
    A. Symonds. TTBB, TB solos. Unac. ACA.

389. KORTE, KARL (1928-   ). Bitter Is My Lot (No. 6
    from the Choral Cycle: Aspects of Love). TT(B)B.
    Unac. Eng. Text: Shao Ch'ang (Ch'ing Dynasty),
    trans. Henry Hart. ECS #2310.

390. KORTE. Jenny Kissed Me, Rondeau (No. 7 from the
    Choral Cycle: Aspects of Love). TB. pf. Eng.
    Text: James Henry Leigh Hunt. ECS #2114.

391. KORTE. Marriage (No. 4 from the Choral Cycle:
    Aspects of Love). TB. pf. Eng. Text: Ralph
    Waldo Emerson. ECS #211.

392. KORTE. May the Sun Bless Us. TB. pf./orch:
    4 hns. 3 tr. 3 tromb. tuba, perc. (2 players),
    timp. Four mvts: (1) I Am Restless. (2) Hiss-
    ing Serpents. (3) When This Is Done. (4) May
    the Sun Bless You. Eng. Text: Rabindranath
    Tagore and the Upanishads. ECS #2317. (12:00).

393. KORTE. Wine of the Grape (No. 5 from the Choral
    Cycle: Aspects of Love). T. solo with pf. Eng.
    Text: Li t'ai Po (T'ang Dynasty). Eng. trans.
    Henry Hart. ECS #2112.

394. KRAEHENBUEHL, DAVID (1932-   ). Four Christmas
    Madrigals. TTBB (SSAA). Unac. Eng. (1) Wel-
    come Yule. (2) I Sing of a Maiden. (3) What
    Cheer. (4) A Christmas Blessing. AMP. Com-
    posed for the Yale Freshman Chorus.

395. KRAFT, LEO (1922-   ). A New Song. TBB. Unac.
    Eng. Text: Ps. 98. MER #MC500-5. Composed
    1964.

396. KRENEK, ERNST (1900-). Four Little Male
      Choruses, op. 32. (Vier kleine Männerchöre nach
      Fragmenten von Hölderlin). TB, A solo. Unac.
      Ger. Text: Hölderlin. UNIV. 10,429.

397. KRENEK. Missa Duodecim Tonorum. TTB. org.
      Lat. Rare instance of a 12-Tone Mass for male
      voices. GI #1001.

398. KUBIK, GAIL (1914-). A Sailor, He Come to Court
      Me. TTBB. Unac. vln. solo. Eng. Text: Bill
      Roberts. MMC #MC306.

399. KUBIK. Choral Profiles: Oliver De Lancey. TB.
      pf. Eng. Text: Stephan Vincent Benét. GS
      #9862.

400. KUBIK. Hop Up, My Ladies (American Folk Song
      Sketch). TTBB. TB solos. vln. solo. Unac.
      Eng. Text: trad. with additional lyrics by Kubik.
      SOU #24-33. Commissioned by the Robert Shaw
      Chorale, 1948.

401. KUBIK. John Henry (American Folk Song Sketch).
      TTBB. pf. Eng. Text: trad. American. RIC
      #1925-14. Commissioned by the Robert Shaw
      Chorale, 1948.

402. KUBIK. Johnny Stiles (American Folk Song Sketch).
      TTBB, B. solos. pf. Eng. Text: trad. with ad-
      ditional lyrics by Kubik. SOU #26-12. Commis-
      sioned by the Robert Shaw Chorale, 1948.

403. KUBIK. Litany and Prayer. TB (some div.) pf.
      reduction of full score. Eng. Text: adap. by
      composer from Episcopal Book of Common Prayer.
      Same Music, different texts: (1) A Service of In-
      tercession for War. (2) A Supplication for Deliver-
      ance from Sin and Guidance in the Ways of Peace.
      SOU #ME 1011. (12:00). Dedicated to the Chorus
      of the U.S. Army Music School, Fort Myer, Vir-
      ginia, 1943-44.

404. KUBIK. The Monotony Song (American Folk Song
      Sketch). TB, B. solo. pf. Eng. Text: Theodore
      Roethke. RIC #1927-15.

405. KURKA, ROBERT (1921-1957). Who Shall Speak for
      the People. TTBB. Unac. Eng. Text: Carl Sand-
      burg. BH #5028.

406. LANGLAIS, JEAN (1907-). Mass God Have Mercy.
      Unis. org. Eng. MCR #2577.

407. LANGLAIS. Missa Dona Nobis Pacem. Unis. org.
      Eng. NOV #2836.

408. LANGLAIS. Missa Salve Regina. TTBB. people's
      unis. chorus. 3 tr. 5 tromb. 2 org. Lat. ECP.
      (18:00).

409. LANGLAIS. Psalm 150. TTB. org. Eng. MCR
      #2203. (3:00).

410. LANGLAIS. The Canticle of the Sun. 3 ev. pf/org.
      (10:00).

411. LASSUS, ORLANDUS (1530-1594). (Also known as
      Orlando di Lasso). 21 motets for 3 and 4 part
      male chorus are available in the collected works of
      Lassus: Orlando di Lasso (Sämtliche Werke), pub.
      BHL. They are also all found in Anthologia Poly-
      phnica (Auctorem Saeculi XVI) Paribus Vocibus, ed.
      Raffaele Casimiri, pub. by Edizione Psalterium,
      Rome. The 21 motets by Lassus and their pagina-
      tion in Casimiri are Adoramus te. TTB(SSA).
      p. 71; Afflictus sum. TTBB. p. 72; Convertere
      Domine. TTBB. p. 74; Cor meum. TTB. p.
      75; Dixi: Confitebor. TTB. p. 78; Eripe me.
      TTB. p. 80; Eipse redimet. TTB. p. 81; Hodie
      apparuit. TTB. p. 83; Inimici autem. TTBB.
      p. 85; In quacumque die. TTB. p. 86; Joannes
      est nommen. TTBB. p. 87; Ne projicias me.
      TTB. p. 90. Quia apud a Dominum. TTB. p.
      92; Quia apud te. TTB. p. 93. Quia detecerunt.
      TTBB. p. 94; Quia dixi. TTB. p. 95. Quoniam
      die ac nocte. TTBB. p. 96; Spiritus tuus. TTBB.
      p. 99. Tibi laus. TTBB. p. 100; Tu exurgens.
      TTB. p. 103; Verbum caro. TTB. p. 58. Also
      see titles (octavos) under Lassus, and the Harvard
      Glee Club Collection. In the collected works see:
      Ad te, perenne gaudium. TTB. I p. 60; Beatus
      vir. TTBB. III p. 50.

68   Music for Men's Voices

412. LASSUS. Cantiones duarum vocum (Magnum opus
     I-XX), ed. Boepple. (12 motets for 2 voices).
     Unac. Lat. MP. (1:00-2:00 ea.).

413. LASSUS. Hodie apparuit (On This Day), ed. May-
     nard Klein. TTB. Unac. Lat. Eng. Text: Un-
     known. GS #11783.

414. LASSUS. Three Psalms, ed. Boepple. TT(B)B. Un-
     ac. Lat. Eng. (1) Psalm 25, Judica me, Domine.
     (2) Psalm 5, Verba mea auribus. (3) Psalm 43,
     Deus auribus nostris. Eng. vers. Harvey Officer.
     MMC #21. (1:00 ea.).

415. LATHAM, WILLIAM P. (1917-). Songs of a Day
     Rome Was Not Built In. TTBB. Unac. Eng.
     Text: Sixth Cent. Latin Poets of Carthage, (#1 by
     Luxorius). Eng. vers. Jack Lindsay. Four set-
     tings: (1) On a Hairy Philosopher. (2) A Kiss.
     (3) A Boozer's Dream. (4) On a Statue of Venus.
     AMP #A655.

416. LE FLEMING, CHRISTOPHER (1908-). Brighten
     Our Darkness (a collect), op. 12, no. 4 TB(SA).
     pf/org. Eng. CHES.

417. LENEL, LUDWIG (1900-). Christ Is Now Risen
     Again. TTBB. Tr. Eng. CON.

418. LEVY, ERNST (1895-?). Hear, Ye Children. TBB-
     TBB. Unac. Eng. Text: Proverbs 4:1, 7, 8.
     ALB #BCS1.

419. LEWANDOWSKI, LOUIS (1821-1894). Ase L'Maan
     (from Cantorial Anthology Vol. I), ed. Ephros.
     TTBB. Unac. Heb. Text: Jewish Liturgical.
     BLOCH.

420. LEWANDOWSKI. V'al Y'de Avodecho, no. 2 (from
     Cantorial Anthology, Vol. I), ed. Ephros. TTBB.
     Unac. Heb. Text: Jewish Liturgical. BLOCH.

421. LISZT, FRANZ. In the BHW complete edition of
     Liszt, see:
     1) Anima Christi. TTBBTTBB. org. Lat.
     2) An den Heiligen Fransiskus Von Paula. TTBB.
        org. (3 tromb, timp. 2d lib). Ger.

3) Ave Maris stella. TTBB. org.
4) Christus est geboren. TTBB. org. Ger.
5) Domine salvum fac regem. TTBB. T solo.
org. Lat. Hoffman von Fallersleben.
6) Mass for Men's Voices. TTBB. org. Lat.
7) Festgesang (Hoffmann von Fallersleben). TTBB.
org. Lat.
8) Mihi autem adhaerere. TTBB. org. Lat.
9) Ossa arrida. TTBB. org. (4 hands). Lat.
10) Pater Noster. TTBB. org. Lat.
11) Pax Vobiscum. TTBB. org. (2d lib). Lat.
12) Requiem Mass for Men's Voices. TTBB. org.
org/2 tr, 2 tromb., timp. Lat.
13) Slavimo, slavno, slaveni. TTBB. org. Magyar
language.
14) Tantum ergo. TTBB. org. Lat.
15) Te Deum laudamus. TTBB. org. Lat.
16) Tu es Petrus. TTBB. org. Lat.

422. LISZT. Eine Faust-Symphonie. TTBB. T solo.
Ger. Text: Goethe. orch: 3232/4331/timp. perc.
org/str. (72:00). Pub. Schuberth.

423. LISZT. Gaudeamus igitur--Humoreske, ed. Erich
Kunzel. TTBB. pf. Lat. Text: trad. Ger.
BH #5408.

424. LISZT. Pax vobiscum (Peace Be with You), ed.
Robert J. Hines. TTBB. pf/org. LGGS #51820.

425. LISZT. Requiem Mass for Male Voices: Requiem
(9:00); Dies irae (15:00); Offertorium (7:00); Sanctus (8:30); Agnus Dei (5:30); Libera (5:00). (tot.
51:00). TTBB. org. Lat. c/o JB.

426. LISZT. Septem sacramenta (responsorien). The
Seven Sacraments, for soli, chorus, org. or harmonium, ed. Imra Sulyok. The Eulenburg Edition (Zurich) includes the original instructions for
org. registration and manuals. TTBB. (#2 has
SA ad lib; #3 and 7 are mainly TTBB, but SA is
obligatory). In 7 sections: 1. Baptisma. 2. Con-
firmatis. 3. Eucharistica. 4. Poenitentia. 5.
Extreme Unctio. 6. Ordo. 7. Matrimonium.
The work was written in 1878 in Rome and was influenced by drawings of the same titles by Friedrick
Overbeck. The first concert performance was July
10, 1879.

70   Music for Men's Voices

427. LEIGHTON, KENNETH (1929-   ).   Three Psalms,
      op. 54. TTBB. Eng. (1) Like as the Hart.
      Text: Ps. 42:3, 6, 12, 13, 15. (2) The Lord Is
      My Shepherd. Text: Ps. 23. (3) Sing Unto the
      Lord a New Song. Text: Ps. 149:3 and Ps. 98:7-
      10. A difficult, but well written work. Dedicated
      to the Baccholian Singers. The composer teaches
      at the University of Edinburgh. NOV #NCM34.

428. LOCKWOOD, NORMAND (1906-   ).   Dirge for Two
      Veterans. TTBB, T solo. pf. Eng. Text: Walt
      Whitman. WB #9W-3438.

429. LOCKWOOD. Prelude to Western Star: Americans
      and Lend Me Your Music. arr. Kunzel. TTBB,
      T solo. pf. Eng. Text: Stephen Vincent Benét.
      BH #434.

430. LOCKWOOD. The Story of St. Nicholas. TTBB, S
      solo. ALA.

431. LOESSER, FRANK (1910-1970). Fugue for Tinhorns
      from Guys and Dolls. TTB. pf. Eng. Text: Loes-
      ser. FMC. (1:30).

432. LOEWE, CARL (1796-1869). Drei Friedrich Rückert-
      Chöre. All for men's chorus, Unac. Ger. (1)
      Das War das Kloster. (2) Mein Hochgebornes
      schatzelein. (3) Seht den Strabstrompeter. LC.

433. LONDON, EDWIN (1927-   ).   The Polonius Platitudes.
      Male chorus and balloons. An avant-garde piece.
      EAM #B132.

434. LONDON. Three Settings of the XXIII Psalm. No. I
      for TTBB. (Also settings for female and mixed
      voices). Unac. Lat. MJQ. Composed 1969.

435. LORA, ANTONIO (1899-1965). Little Boy Alone.
      TTBB. Unac. Eng. Text: G. Snyder. ACA.

436. LORA. Storm. TTBB. Unac. Eng. Text: Gratia
      Snyder. ACA.

437. LOTTI, ANTONIO (1667-1740). Mass for Two Vocum
      Aequalium (Two Equal Voices). TB. Unac. Lat.
      Gloria, Kyrie, with Sanctus, Benedictus, Agnus Dei,
      by B. Cordans (1700-1757). AB.

438. LOTTI. Mass for Three Equal Voices. TTB. Unac. Lat. GIA. Also AB, ECS #566.

439. LOTTI. Vere languores nostros (Surely He Hath
Borne Our Griefs), ed. Hunter. TTB. Unac.
Eng. Lat. Text: Isaiah 53:4, 5. EBM #4458.
Also, ECS #40; RIC #SY130. (2:30).

440. LOVELACE, AUSTIN (1919-). Christmas Night.
TTBB. Unac. Eng. Text: Marion Lockhead.
JF #9927-4. (1:20).

441. LOVELACE. God Who Created Me. TB, with boys
choir. pf/org. Eng. Text: H. C. Beeching.
CF #7149.

442. LUENING, OTTO (1900-). The Tiger Ghost.
TTBB. Unac. Eng. Text: Swenson. ACA.
(3:30).

443. LUYTHON, KAREL (1558-1620). Missa Quodlibetica,
ed. A. Smijers. TTBB. Unac. Lat. WL.

444. MACDOWELL, EDWARD. He also used the pseudonym
"Edgar Thorn." A file on Mac Dowell's male choral
music is at the NY Public Library.

445. MACHAUT, GUILLAUME DE (c. 1300-1377). Messe
de Nôtre (Nostre) Dame, ed. Jacques Chailley.
TTBB. Unac. Lat. SAL.

446. MALIPIERO, G. FRANCESCO (1882-1973). Universa
Universis. TB. and inst. acc: 2202/4000/pf/20042.
(Tot. 19 instruments). Lat. Text: Medieval Goliard Lyrics. Composed for the Venice Celebration
of 1942. SZ. (19:00).

447. MARCELLO, BENEDETTO (1686-1739). And with
Songs I Will Celebrate, ed. Richard Wienhorst.
TB (SA). org. (pf). Text: Ps. 13:6. Eng. adap.
Stevens. CON #98-1047. (2:30).

448. MARCELLO. Psalm X (TB); Psalm XIV (BB); Psalm
XXV (TB); Psalm XXII (TT); Psalm XLII (B); and
Psalm XXX (TB) from Estro Poetico-Armonico (50
Psalms). The paraphrases were the work of Girol-
amo Giustiniani. Originally published at Venice be-
tween 1724 and 1726, this anthology was also issued

72   Music for Men's Voices

in an Eng. trans. edition by Avison and Garth in
1757. GP. DC.

449. MARCELLO. Oh, Hold Thou Me Up, ed. Wienhorst.
TB(SA). org. Eng. Text: Ps. 17:5, 6. adap.
Stevens. CON #98-1046. (4:00).

450. MARCELLO. O Lord, Deliver Me, ed. Wienhorst.
TTBB. Text: Ps. 8:1-2. Eng. adap. Stevens.
CON #98-1044. (2:00).

451. MARLOW, RICHARD. The Preces and Responses.
TTBB. Unac. OX #5599. Written for the Pre-
centor and Choir of Trinity College, Cambridge.

452. MARTINI, GIOVANNI BATTISTA (1706-1784). In
monte oliveti, ed. Rev. Walter Williams. TTBB.
Unac. Lat. Text: Matt. 26:39, 41. Eng. Williams.
ECS #1234. Also, RIC #SY113.

453. MARTINŮ, BOHUSLAV (1890-1959). Field Mass
(Olni Mše). Also known as Military Mass. TTBB.
B solo. Instrumentation: 2 fl; (picc.); 2 cl. in
B-Flat, 3 tr. in C, timp. gr. cassa; piatti; tamburo
piccolo (Con corda and senza timbro); tambura military cratolo; triangle; Mass Bells (ad lib.); harmonium; pf. Slovak. Text: Ps. 44, 42, and original words by Jiri Mucha. On rental. Miltant-
rich, Prague. BH. (20:00). An English translation was made for the Princeton University Chapel
Choir. Recording available: "Field Mass," Chorus
of the Vit Nejedly Army Ensemble and soloists of
the Czech Philharmonic. Supraphon #SUA 10387.

454. MARTINŮ. The Prophecy of Isaiah. TTBB, SAB
solos. orch: Timp. tr. va. pf. Eng. Heb. Text:
Isaiah XXIV:1-8, 10-12, 16-23 and XXI: 1-4, 13,
15-17. Martinů's last composition, composed between 1954-1959. Dedicated to the people of Israel.
First performance, Jerusalem, 1963. L.

455. MARTIRANO, SALVATORE (1927-). O, O, O,
That Shakespearian Rag. Taken from a large
scale work. Pt. III for TTBB, cl, A sax, tr,
tromb, strb, pf, perc. (1 player). Eng. Text:
The Tempest, Shakespeare. SCHOTT (LON) #10726.

The Catalog					73

456.	MASSENET, JULES (1842-1912). Choeur des Ro-
	mains from Herodiade. TTBB. HEU.

457.	MASSENET. La Carvane Perdue. TTBB. Unac.
	HEU.

458.	MASSENET. Villanelle. TTBB. Unac. HEU.

459.	MATHIAS, WILLIAM (1934-). Communion Service
	in C, op. 36. Unis. org. OX #5586.

460.	MATHIAS. Gloria, op. 52. TTBB. org. Lat. OX
	#A285. (6:00). Commissioned by the Pontarddu-
	lais Male Choir with funds provided by The Welsh
	Arts Council.

461.	MATHIAS. O Salutaris hostia, op. 48. TTBB. Un-
	ac. Lat. OX #M18. Commissioned by The Welsh
	Arts Council.

462.	MAWBY, COLIN (1938-). O Come, Let Us Sing
	Unto the Lord. 2 ev. org. Eng. (1) Ps. 95, vs.
	1-5; (2) Ps. 137, vs. 1-4; (3) Ps. 101, 1-4; (4)
	Ps. 148, vs. 1-5. GI #1098.

463.	MAYUZUMI, TOSHIRO (1929-). Nirvana Symphony
	(Buddhist Cantata). 12 part male chorus. orch:
	6363/6361/Timp. 6 percussion players, hp. pf.
	cel/str. CFP #P6336. In Buddhist language (score
	indications, directions in Fr.). (35:00). Com-
	posed 1958.

464.	MAYUZUMI. Prtidesana, a Buddhist Cantata. 6
	part male chorus, TBB solos. 3 hns, timp. 4
	perc. players, 2 pf. CFP #P6892. (27:00). Com-
	posed 1963.

465.	McBRIDE, ROBERT (1911-). Sir Patrick Spence.
	Men's Voices. ACA. (5:00).

466.	McKINNEY, HOWARD (1890-). Collegiarum Car-
	mina. A Choral fantasy based on American college
	songs. TTBB. (SATB). pf. Eng. JF #9658.
	(10:00).

467.	McPHEE, COLIN (1901-). Sea Chanty Suite. TTBB.

2 pf. 6 timp. (2 players.) Eng. McPhee is an expert on the music of Bali. Music out of print, but a score is available at the New York Public Library at Lincoln Center. Also, try KAL. (20:00).

468. MECHEM, KIRKE (1925-). English Girls, op. 39, nos. 1, 2, 3. (1) Jenny Kissed Me. Text: Leigh Hunt. (2) Julia's Voice. Text: Robert Herrick. (3) To Celia. Text: Ben Johnson, from Volpone, Act III, Sc. 7. All TBB. pf. Eng. BH #5856, 7, 8.

469. MECHEM. Three American Folk Songs, op. 6, nos. 1, 2, 3. All TTBB. pf. Eng. (1) Aunt Rudy. (2) Wayfaring Stranger. (3) Blue Tail Fly. ECS #2313, 4, 5.

470. MELLERS, WILFRID. Chants and Litanies of Carl Sandburg. TB (some div.). pf. perc. Eng. Text: Carl Sandburg. NOV.

471. MENDELSSOHN, FELIX (1809-1847). Antigone, op. 55. TTBB-TTBB. pf. Eng. Text: W. Bartholomew, after Sophocles. NOV. Also JB #492. Composed in 1841. Orch: 2222/2230/timp. harp/ str.

472. MENDELSSOHN. Beati mortui, ed. Hines. Eng. LG #51707.

473. MENDELSSOHN. Der Jäger Abschied (The Hunter's Farewell), ed. Clough-Leighter. TTBB. Unac. Ger. Eng. Text: Josef von Eichendorff. ECS #559. Also GS #4992. Eng. vers. Clarence Alvord.

474. MENDELSSOHN. Festgesang an die Künstler (Festival Ode), op. 68. TTBB-TTBB (solo quartet). Brass: 4 hns. 4 tr. 3 tromb. Bar. tuba. Ger. Text: Schiller. Eng. Trans. Robert A. Hall, Jr. RK #615. Also JB #1210. (7:30). "Mendelssohn wrote two works under the title Festgesang. The later (1846) title is to a text by Schiller; the earlier (1840) was written for the Gutenburg Festival for male chorus and double orchestra of brass instruments. It is published by Broude Brothers as Festival Hymns on the Printing of the Bible. The

second mvt. melody is the source of the carol,
"Hark, the Herald Angels Sing."

475. MENDELSSOHN. Lieder für Männerstimmen (Songs
for Men's Voices). All in Ger. (1) Türkisches
Schenkenlied, op. 50, no. 1. TTBB. Unac. Text:
Goethe. (2:00). (2) Der Jäger Abschied, op. 50,
no. 2. TTBB. 4 hns. tromb. Text: Eichendorff.
(3) Sommerlied, op. 50, no. 3. TTBB. (Soli)--
TTBB. Unac. Text: Goethe. (2:00). (4) Was-
serfahrt, op. 50, no. 4. TTBB. Unac. Text:
Heine. (3:00). (5) Liebe und Wein, op. 50, no. 5.
TTBB. B solo. Unac. Text: Unknown. (3:00).
(6) Wanderlied, op. 50, no. 6. TTBB (Soli)--
TTBB. Unac. Text: Eichendorff. (2:00). (7)
Der Frohe Wandersmann, op. 75, no. 1. TTBB.
Unac. Text: Eichendorff. (8) Abendständchen,
op. 75, no. 3. TTB. Unac. Text: Goethe.
(1:00). (9) Trinklied, op. 75, no. 3. TTB. Unac.
Text: Goethe. (1:00). (10) Das Lied vom Braven
Mann, op. 76, no. 4. TTBB. Unac. Text: H.
Fallersleben. (12) Beati mortui, op. 115, no. 1.
TTBB. Unac. Lat. Text: Apocalypse 14:13. (13)
Periti autem, op. 115, no. 2. TTBB. Unac.
Lat. Eng. Text: Dan. 12:3, 4. and Matt. 3:43.
(14) Jaglied, op. 120, no. 1. TTBB. (Soli)--
TTBB. Unac. Text: Scott. (1:00). (15) Im
Süden, op. 120, no. 2. TTBB. Unac. Text:
Unknown. (2:00). (16) Zigeunerlied, op. 120, no.
4. TTBB. Unac. Text: Goethe.
(2:00). (17) Ersatz für Unterstand. TTBB. (Soli)--
TTBB. Unac. Text: Rückert. (4:00). CFP
#1772.

476. MENDELSSOHN. The Righteous Living Forever (Periti autem). op. 115, no. 1. TTBB. pf. Lat.
Eng. Text: adap. from Dan. 12:3, 4. and Matt.
13:43. NOV #255. (2:00). Also CF. Op. 115,
no. 2. is Beati mortui, to be found in Lieder für
Männerstimmen, and as a separate octavo.

477. MENDELSSOHN. Say, Where Is He That Is Born
King of Judah from Christus. TBB. org. Eng.
Text: adap. Glasser, from Matt. 2:2. ECS #1611.

478. MENDELSSOHN. Zwei Geistliche Chor, op. 115.
TTBB. Unac. (1) Beati Mortui, op. 115, no. 1

(Wie Selig sind die Töten). (2) Periti Autem, op.
115, no. 2. (Es strahlen Hill die Gerechten).
BHW.

479. MEYEROWITZ, JAN (1913-). Two choruses on
      Poems by A. E. Housman. TTBB. Fr. Hn.
      Eng. (1) Stone, Steel Dominions, Pass. (2) The
      Farms of Home. BRBR.

480. MILHAUD, DARIUS (1892-1974). Agamemnon. TTBB,
      (some div.), S solo. pf. 4 hands. Fr. Text: Paul
      Claudel. Publishers: Heugel, Paris, c/o TP.

481. MILHAUD. Psalm 121. TTBB. Unac. Fr. Eng.
      Ger. Text: Paul Claudel. UN #9632. Dedicated
      to the Harvard Glee Club, 1921.

482. MILLS, CHARLES (1914-). The Constant Lover.
      TTBB. Unac. Eng. Text: Sir John Suckling. ACA.

483. MILLS. Why So Pale and Wan. TTBB. Unac. Text:
      Sir John Suckling. ACA.

484. MITCHELL, LYNDOL (1923-1964). St. Mark's Easter
      Gospel. TTBB. org. 3 tr. ad lib. TP #312-
      40631. (6:30).

485. MOE, DANIEL (1926-). I Will Extol Thee. TTBB.
      Unac. Eng. Text: Ps. 145. AUG #PS. 623.

486. MOEVS, ROBERT (1920-). Cantata sacra. TTBB.
      Bar. solo. fl. 3 tromb. timp. (2 picc., 1 grande
      autom). Lat. In 4 mvts: (1) Introit, 4th Sunday
      after Easter, Cantate Domino, Ps. 97:1-2. (2) Al-
      leluia, 4th Sunday after Easter, Dextera Dei, Ps.
      117:16. (3) Offertory, Easter Sunday, Terra Tre-
      muit, Ps. 75:9, 10. (4) Communion, 5th Sunday
      after Easter, Cantate Domino, Ps. 95:2. ACL.

487. MOHLER, PHILIPP. Laetare. Male chorus, T
      solo. Orch, org. or piano, 4 hands. Ger. Writ-
      ten for the 1968 festival of the Deutschen Sänger-
      bundes. Thematic material from the Gregorian in-
      troit, "Laetare" and the Chorale, "Christ is Risen"
      Schotts, Mainz (AMP). (15:00).

488. MONNIKENDAM, MARIUS (1896-1977). Magnificat.

TTBB, S solo. 2 pf. and perc. (Also available for SATB). Text: Luke 1:46-56. CFP. Composed 1966.

489. MONTEVERDI, CLAUDIO (1567-1648). Angelus ad pastores ait, ed. Boepple. 3 ev. Unac. Lat. Text: Luke 2:10-11 (Christmas Day, Third Antiphon, Lauds). MMC #24. (1:00).

490. MONTEVERDI. As from the Earth a Flower Grows (canzonetta), arr. Herbert Zipper. TTB(SSA). Unac. EBM #45. (2:30).

491. MONTEVERDI. Deus tuorum militum. TBB. str. Lat. OX #41.028.

492. MONTEVERDI. Hodie Christus natus est, ed. Boepple. 3 ev. Unac. Lat. Text: Christmas Day, Antiphon, Magnificat. MMC #24. Also FC #NY2041. (1:30).

493. MONTEVERDI. Sacrae Cantiunculae. 3 eq. voices. MM #MC24.

494. MONTEVERDI. Veni, sponsa Christi (Come, Thou Faithful Servant), ed. Vené. TTB. Unac. Lat. Eng. Text: Matt. 25:34. RIC #NY20332.

495. MOORE, DOUGLAS (1893-1970). Simon Legree. TTBB, Bar. solo. pf. Eng. Text: Vachel Lindsay. CF #CM2230.

496. MORALES, CHRISTOBAL DE (1500-1530). Agnus Dei from Missa L'Homme Armé, ed. Leo Kraft. TTB. Unac. Lat. Text: Mass. MMC #MC359. (2:30).

497. MORALES. Missa Ave Maria, ed. E. Bruning. TTBB. Unac. Lat. Text: Mass. WL.

498. MORLEY, THOMAS (1557-1603). I Go Before My Charmer (canzonetta), ed. G. W. Woodworth. TB(SA). Unac. Eng. Text: Anon. ECS #824. (1:15).

499. MORLEY. Round, Around About a Wood, ed. Elliot Forbes. TTBB. Unac. Eng. Text: Anon. GS #10745.

500. MORLEY. Say, Dear, Will You Not Have Me, ed.
     Forbes. TBB. Unac. Eng. Text: Anon. GS
     #10746.

501. MOUSSORGSKY, MODESTE (1839-1881). Four Rus-
     sian Love Songs. TTBB. Unac. T solo in #1.
     2T solos in #4. Text: Eng. Roger Maren. EBM
     #54.

502. MOUSSORGSKY. Khovanstchina: Act II, Sc. I,
     L'Heresie and Act III, Sc. VI, Ah, nul chagrin.
     TTBB. pf. Fr. Eng. vers. Rosa Newmarch.
     Publishers: Breitkopf und Härtel.

503. MOZART, WOLFGANG AMADEUS. (1756-1791). Die
     Maurerfreuden, KV 471. TTB, T solo. pf. Ger.
     Text: Franz Petran. BHW #5929. Orch: 2 ob.
     1 cl, 2 hns, str. Composed 1785.

504. MOZART. Dir, Seele des Weltalls, KV 429. TTB,
     S solo. pf. Ger. Text: Unknown. BHW #429.
     Composed 1783. Orch: 2 vl. va. 2 ob. Bn.

505. MOZART. Eine Kleine Freimaurerkantate, KV 623.
     TTB, TB solos. pf. Ger. Text: Emmanuel Schi-
     kaneder. BHW #5930. Orch: 1 fl. 2 ob. 2 hns.
     str.

506. MOZART. Idomeneo: Pietà, numi pietà, (Act I).
     TTBB-TTBB. pf. It. Text: Giammatteo Varesco.

507. MOZART. Magic Flute: Three Choruses (1) O Isis,
     Schenket der Weisheit Geist. (2) Bewaret Euch.
     (3) O Isis, Welche Wonne. TTBB, B solo. pf.
     Text: Eng. Cleveland Jauch. Ger. E. Schikaneder
     and Gieseke. HF. (3:00 ea.).

508. MOZART. Zwei Prater-Kannons (Two Kannons). 4
     ev. Unac. Ger. Text: Mozart. VLD.

509. MUELLER, CARL F. (1892-). Laudamus Te (Holy
     God We Praise Thy Name). TTBB. Unac. Eng.
     GS #8514.

510. NANINO, GIOVANNI (1545-1607). Hodie Christus
     natus est. TTBB. Unac. Lat. Text: Christmas
     Day, Antiphon, Magnificat, 2nd Vespers. CF #2809.

511. NEHLYBEL, VACLAV (1919-). Come, O My Love,
     from Four Ballads. TBB. Unac. Eng. Text:
     Trad. FC #NY2601-8.

512. NELSON, RON (1929-). Behold Man. TTBB. Un-
     ac. Eng. Text: Albert van Nostrand. BH #5403.

513. NELSON. Meditation on the Syllably OM. TTBB,
     TB solos. Unac. Eng. Text: James Schevill.
     BH #5809. (6:18).

514. NEWBURY, KENT (1925-). Psalm 150. TTBB.
     Unac. Eng. Text: Ps. 150. LGGS. Dedicated to
     the Miami Univ. (Oxford, Florida) Men's Glee Club.

515. NIELAND, JAN (1903-). Prayer of St. Francis.
     TB. org. Text: St. Francis. WL #ESA 512-2.

516. NIELSEN, CARL (1865-1931). 17 Songs. For Male
     Voices. Unac. Danish Text: Pub. Wilhelm Hansen.
     Copenhagen.

517. NILES, JOHN JACOB (1892-). Curtains of Night.
     TTBB, T solo. Unac. Eng. Text: Niles. MF
     #1054.

518. NILES. Venezuela. TTBB. pf. Eng. Text: Niles.
     CF #CM 6663. (2:15).

519. NORDEN, HUGO (1909-). O Satisfy Us With They
     Mercy. TTBB. Unac. Eng. Text: from Ps. 90-
     ABIN #APM-406.

520. NOSS, LUTHER (1907-). Psalms and Hymns of
     Early America, in 3 Vols. Vol. I: Two Tunes
     from the Ainsworth Psalter. (1) By Babels River,
     Ps. 137. (2) O Praise Jah, Ps. 150. Vol. II:
     Three Tunes from the Bay Psalm Book. (1) Hark-
     en, O God, Ps. 61:1-4, 8. (2) O God, to Rescue
     Me, Ps. 70. (3) Yee Heav'ns of Heav'ns, Ps.
     148:1-9. Vol. III: Two Tunes from the Missouri
     Harmony. (1) Through Ev'ry Age, Ps. 90, para-
     phrased by Isaac Watts. (2) Glorious Things of
     Thee, by John Newton. All for TBB. Unac.
     AMP #A224, A226, A227.

521. NOWAK, LIONEL (1911-). Wisdom Exalteth Her

Children. TBB-TBB (SSA-SSA). Unac. Eng. Text:
Ecclesiastes 4:11-12. ALB #BC52. (3:15).

522. OFFENBACH, JACQUES (1819-1880). La Belle Hé-
      lène: Bacchanale. TTB. pf. Fr. Text: Meilhac
      and Halevy. GS #9799. (2:00).

523. OFFENBACH. Tales of Hoffmann: Drig, Drig, Drig
      and Il était une fois. TTB. pf. Gr. Text: Bar-
      bier. KAL #6363. (2:30).

524. ORFF, CARL (1895-). Carmina Burana: In Ta-
      berna (Part II). (The entire part II is effective
      as a unit). TTBB. pf. TB solos. Lat. Text:
      13th Cent. Student Songs. (1) Estuans interius.
      solo Bar. no chorus. (2:00). (2) Olim lacus
      colueram. solo T. TBB. (3:30). (3) Ego sum
      abbas. solo Bar. TTBB. (2:30). (4) In taberna
      quando sumas. TBB. (3:30). SCH.

525. ORFF. Carmina Burana: Cours d'Amours (Part III),
      Si puer cum puella. TTTBBB. pf. Lat. Text:
      13 Cent. Student Song. SCH. (1:00).

526. ORFF. Sunt lacrimae rerum from Concerto di voci.
      BBBBB (or TTTBBB). TBB solos. Unac. Lat.
      (1) Omnium deliciarum. Text: Orlando di Lasso.
      (2) Omnia tempus habent. Text: Ecclesiastes
      3:1-8. (3) Eripe nos. Text: trans. Rudolf Bach.
      SCH #39 534. (13:00). There is also a revised
      version of 1957.

527. ORFF. Two Three Part Choruses: 1. Von der
      Freundlichkeit der Welt (Auf die Erde noller kaltam
      Wind). Ger. Text: Bertold Brecht. 2. Aufruf
      (Komm sint Plut der Seele). Ger. Text: Franz
      Werfel. Both TBB. Unac. 3 pf. perc. SCH.
      (15:00).

528. ORFF. Vom Frühjahr, Öltank und vom Fliegen. A
      cantata of three movements to a text by Bertold
      Brecht. First two are for male chorus: (1) On
      Spring. (2) Seven Hundred Intellectuals Pray to an
      Oiltank. 6 percussionists. Eng. Ger. SCHOTT
      #6023.

529. OVERTON, HALL (1920-). Captivity. TTB. Eng.
      Text: Chaucer. ACA. (4:00).

PALESTRINA, GIOVANNI PIERLUIGI DA (1524-1594).
Many motets, some originally for TTBB, others
for ATTB, can be found in the collected works:
Palestrina's Werke. pub. by Breitkopf und Härtel,
or the Anthologia Polyphonica by Casimiri. Many
Sections of the 35 Magnificats and Masses are
scored for equal low voices.

530. PALESTRINA. Assumpta est Maria, ed. Boepple.
      TTB (SSA). Unac. (Instr: str., winds or brass).
      Lat. Text: Antiphon, Vespers, Assumption. MMC
      #MC1. (4:25).

531. PALESTRINA. Ave Maria, arr. Harman. TTBB.
      Unac. Lat. Text: Luke 1:28. HF. (3:30).

532. PALESTRINA. Benedictus from the Missa Brevis,
      ed. Ruggero Vené. TTB(SSA). Unac. Lat. Eng.
      Text: Harold Heiberg. FC #NY2185.

533. PALESTRINA. Benedictus from Mass, Repleatur os
      meum laude, ed. Leo Kraft. TTB(SSA). Unac.
      Lat. Text: Mass. MMC #MC352. (3:00).

534. PALESTRINA. Supplicationes, ed. G. Wallace Wood-
      worth. TTB. Unac. Lat. Text: Lamentations of
      Jeremiah. GS #9798.

535. PEETERS, FLOR (1903-). Entrata festiva. Unis.
      2 tr. 2 tromb. org. Lat. Text: attr. Charlemagne.
      CFP #6159. (7:00).

536. PEETERS. Jubilate Deo, op. 40. TTB. org. Lat.
      Eng. Text: Ps. 99. MCR #1893. (9:00).

537. PEETERS. Magnificat. TTB. org. Lat. Text:
      Luke 1:46-56. MCR #2527.

538. PEETERS. Missa in Honorem Reginae Pacis. TB.
      org. Lat. MCR #1692. (18:00).

539. PEETERS. Missa in Honorem Sancti Lutgardis. TB.
      org. Lat. MCR #1758. (20:00).

540. PEETERS. Te Deum. TT(B)B. org. Lat. Eng.
      Text: Nicetas, Bishop, ca. 400. MCR #1484. (5:00).

541. PEETERS. The Confraternity Mass. Unis. org.
      Eng. MCR #2568.

542. PEPUSCH, JOHN (1667-1752). Fill Every Glass
     from The Beggar's Opera. TB. pf. T solo.
     Text: John Gay. HB #1403. (1:15).

543. PEPUSCH. Let Us Take the Road from The Beggar's
     Opera, arr. Austin. TTBB. pf. T solo. Eng.
     Text: John Gay. BH #1403. (1:15).

544. PEROSI, LORENZO (1872-1956). Missa Te Deum
     Laudamus. TB. org. Lat. RIC.

545. PEROTINUS (ca. 1200). (Also called PEROTIN).
     Organum Quadruplum: Sederunt principes, arr.
     Rudolf Fricker, for men's chorus and boys' or
     women's chorus and orch: 3 ob. 3 bn. 2 tr. 2
     tromb. bells. triangle. va. VE #8211. (15:00).

546. PERSICHETTI, VINCENT (1915-   ).   Four Cummings
     Choruses, op. 98. TB. pf. Eng. Text: e. e.
     cummings. (1) Dominic Has a Doll. (2) Nouns
     to Nouns. (3) Maggie and Milly and Molly and
     May. (4) Uncles. EVC #1222, 3, 4, 5. (6:00
     tot.).

547. PERSICHETTI. Jimmie's Got a Goil. TB. pf.
     4 hands. Text: e. e. cummings. GS #9800.
     (3:00). A Juilliard Commission.

548. PERSICHETTI. Sam Was a Man. TB. pf. Eng.
     Text: e. e. cummings. GS #9791. (3:00).

549. PERSICHETTI. Song of Peace. TTBB. pf. (org.).
     Eng. Text: Anon. EVC #130. (3:00).

550. PFAUTSCH, LLOYD (1921-   ). Advent Carol. TTBB.
     Unac. LGGS #51014.

551. PFAUTSCH. Go and Tell John. TTBB. Unac.
     Eng. Text: Matt. 2:4-6. SOM #MM 9007.

552. PHILLIPS, BURILL (1907-   ). That Time May
     Cease. TTBB. pf. Eng. TP #312-40675.

553. PINKHAM, DANIEL (1923-   ). Mass of the Good
     Shepherd. Unis. org. Eng. IONE.

554. PINKHAM. Missa l'Asaph. TBB. instr. ensemble.
     ECS #2316.

555. PINKHAM. Te Deum. TB(SA). 3 tr. B-flat, org.
      Eng. trans. John Dryden. RK #613. (4:30).

556. PISK, PAUL (1893-). Psalm XXX. TTBB. Unac.
      Eng. SOU #ME 1012.

557. PISTON, WALTER (1894-1976). Carnival Song. TBB.
      pf. 4 hands or brass: 3 tr. C, 3 hns. F, 3 tromb.
      tuba. It. Text: DeMedici. ARP #A296. (8:00).
      Composed for the Harvard Glee Club, 1940.

558. PITFIELD, THOMAS (1903-). A Sketchbook for
      Men. (1) Introduction. (2) The Motor Mechanic.
      (3) The Poet. (4) The Policeman. (5) The Com-
      poser. (6) The Singer. (7) The Old Man. (8)
      The Politician. (9) The Preacher. (10) The Farm-
      er's Lad. (11) The Company Director. (12) Con-
      clusion. TBB. Bar. solo. pf. opt. perc. (or
      str. pf. perc.). Eng. Text: Pitfield. CFP #268.
      (25:00).

559. PITFIELD. Evening Service for Men's Voices: Mag-
      nificat and Nunc dimittis. TTBB. org. Eng.
      Text: Luke I:46-56 and Song of Simeon, Luke
      2:29-32. CFP #882.

560. PITFIELD. Miniatures: (1) The Village Bell. (2)
      The Needle. (3) The Windmill. 2 ev. pf. opt.
      perc. (glockenspiel, chime bars or bells). Eng.
      Text: Pitfield. CFP #266A. (1:00 ea.).

561. PITFIELD. Two Metrical Psalms. (1) Ps. 23 (para-
      phrased by Addison). (2) Ps. 127. Unis. pf. or
      org. Eng. CFP #H556B. (4:00, 2:30).

562. PITONI, GUISEPPE (1657-1743). Cantate Domino
      (O Sing Ye to the Lord), ed. Norman Greyson.
      TTBB. Unac. Lat. Eng. Text: Ps. 95. BOU
      #ES56.

563. PITONI. Missa in Nativitatae. TTBB. Unac. Lat.
      CHES.

564. PIZETTI, ILDEBRANDO (1880-1968). Per Un Morto.
      TTBB. It. Fr. RIC #120225.

565. PONCE, JUAN (16th Cent.). Ave color vini clari,
      ed. Goodale. TTBB. Unac. Lat. Eng. Text:

         student drinking song; The Court of Ferdinand and
         Isabella. GS #11082.

566. POOLER, FRANK. Gird Yourself with Lamentations.
         TTBB(SSAA). Unac. Eng. Text: Book of Joel.
         SOM #MM9009.

567. POULENC, FRANCIS (1899-1963). Several male
         Poulenc choruses, "Songs for Tipplers, Monks and
         Patriots" are recorded by the Whikenhard Chorale,
         Lyrichord #LL 7208. Chanson à boire. TTBB.
         Unac. Fr. Text: Jean Victor Hugo. SAL. (3:30).
         Composed 1922.

568. POULENC. Clic, clac. Dansez Sabots, from Chan-
         sons Françaises (Mvt. IV). TTB. Unac. Fr.
         Text: Jean Victor Hugo. Eng. Norman Luboff.
         SAL. (3:30). Composed 1945.

569. POULENC. La Belle si nous étions. TTBB. Unac.
         Fr. Folk. SAL. (1:15). Composed 1948.

570. POULENC. Laudes de Saint Antoine de Padoue. (1)
         O Jesu. (1:45). (2) O Proles. (0:45). (3) Laus
         regi. (2:00). (4) Si quaeris. (2:00). TBB. Un-
         ac. Fr. Text: St. Anthony. SAL. Composed
         1957-59.

571. POULENC. Quatre Prières de Saint Francois d'As-
         sise. (1) Salut, Dame Sainte. TBB. (2:00).
         (2) Tout Puissant, très Saint. TTBB. (1:15).
         (3) Seigneur, je vous en prie. TBB. (1:15).
         (4) O mes très chers frères. TTBB. T solo.
         (1:15). All Unac. Fr. Text: St. Francis of As-
         sisi. Eng. Robert Hess. SAL. Composed 1948.

572. POULENC. Sept répons des Ténèbres. Although
         written for male voice, the work requires boys'
         voices. It is difficult to extract all-male sections;
         nevertheless, it is an interesting work. Lat. SAL.
         Composed 1961.

573. POWER, LEONEL (d. 1445). Ave Regina Caelorum,
         ed. Denis Stevens. ATB solos and men. BR.

574. POWER. Gloria, ed. Margaret Bent. TTBB. Unac.
         OX #EM9.

575. PRAETORIUS, MICHAEL (1571-1621). In Peace and
      Joy (Mit Fried 'und Freud), ed. Hewitt Pantaleoni.
      TTB. Unac. Text: Ger. Paraphrase of Nunc
      dimittis (Luke 2:29-32) by Martin Luther. Eng.
      Pantaleoni. ONC #98-1715.

576. PRAETORIUS. Three Christmas Carols from Musae
      Sioniae, Vol. IX, ed. William Tortolano. 3 ev.
      Unac. GIZ #1944.

577. PURCELL, HENRY (1659-1695). Catches for Men's
      Voices, ed. Dalton. OX #51.030.

578. PURCELL. O, I'm Sick of Life, cont. realized
      Arnold Goldsborough. TTB, org. Eng. Text:
      George Sandys. NOV #PSR 13.

579. PURCELL. Plunged in the Confines of Despair, ed.
      Franklin Zimmerman. TTBB. cont. Eng. Text:
      Ps. 130, paraphrase. SP C195.

580. PURCELL. Sound the Trumpet. TB(SA). pf. Eng.
      Dutch. Text: Unknown. Ed. Musico, The Hague,
      c/o WL. (0:45).

581. PURCELL. The Three Fairies, ed. H. Clough-
      Leighter. TTB. Unac. Eng. Text: Anon. ECS
      #535.

582. QUILTER, ROGER (1877-1953). Non nobis Domine.
      TB. pf. Eng. Text: Rudyard Kipling. BH
      #MFS348.

583. REGER, MAX (1873-1916). Extensive quantity of
      choral music for men's voices. See his collected
      works, pub. Breitkopf und Härtel, Wiesbaden.
      Several works of interest are the following, with
      orch: op. 21, Hymne ad den Gesang; op. 119,
      Weihe der Nacht; op. 126, Römischer Triumphge-
      sang. Some Unac. works of interest: op. 38,
      Sieben Männerchöre; op. 83, Zehn Gesänge für
      Männerchöre; Zwölf Madrigale; Minnelied, op. 83,
      no. 7, available from WIT 2715.

584. REGER. Männerchor, op. 83, nos. 2, 3, 4, 6, 7.
      Lieblich hat sich gesellet. 3. Abendständchen.
      4. Husarenmarsch. 6. Eine gantz neu Schelmeweys.

7. Minnelied. BB. Reger wrote much fine music
for male voices. Almost all unpublished. Of special interest is his Requiem for Male voices. The
best source is his collected works, pub. BHW.
(Vol. 27 for unaccompanied and Vol. 30 for accompanied).

585. RIDOUT, ALAN (1934-). Sequence. Unis. Org.
Eng. Trans: Roy Campbell, from St. John of the
Cross. SB #612.

586. RIEGGER, WALLINGFORD (1885-1951). Evil Shall
Not Prosper. TBB-TBB. Unac. Eng. Text: Wisdom 7:29-30. ALB #BCS3. (6:50). Commissioned
by Bennington College, 1957.

587. RIEGGER. Men of Harlech. TTBB. FLAM #C5014.

588. RIMSKY-KORSAKOV, NICOLAI (1855-1908). Chorus
of Warriors from The Legend of Kitezh, ed. Fitzgerald. TTBB. pf. Text: Eng. vers. Bernard
Fitzgerald. FC #NY1478.

589. ROGERS, BERNARD (1892-1968). Psalm 18. TTBB.
T solo. pf. Eng. TP #312-40600. Commissioned by the University of Rochester Men's Glee Club.
(7:00).

590. ROREM, NED (1923-). A Sermon on Miracles.
Solo voice, unis. chorus and strings: vln. 1 and
2, va. vc. stb. (keyboard). "The work should be
sung either by a male choir with a female soloist
or female choir with a male soloist." Eng. Text:
Paul Goodman. BH. (6:00). Composed at Tangle-
wood, 1947.

591. ROREM. I Feel Death. TBB. Unac. Eng. Text:
John Dryden. BH #5624. (1:00). Composed in
1953.

592. ROREM. Proper for Votive Mass of the Holy Spirit.
Unis. org. Eng. Text: Ps. 103:30 and Stephen
Langton. (1) Entrance Song. (2) Gradual (Medita-
tion Song). (3) Offertory. (4) Communion. Com-
missioned by the Church Music Ass. of America.
BH #5618. (9:00).

593. ROSENMÜLLER, JOHANN (1620-1684). Since the

World is Only Passing, ed. Richard Peek. Unis. pf. Eng. Text: Unknown. CON #98-1820.

594. ROSSINI, GIOACCHINO (1792-1868). Chant Funèbre, ed. Kurt Stone. Composed in 1864 upon the death of Giacomo Meyerbeer. TTBB. T. drum. Fr. Eng. Text: Anon. JB #103. (4:00).

595. ROSSINI. William Tell: Coro di cacciatori e di svizzeri (Chorus of Hunters and Swiss), Act II. TTBB. pf. B solo. It. Hunters' Chorus, men only; Swiss chorus includes S and A parts which can be deleted. Text: based on Schiller novel. BH.

596. ROSSINI. Mille grazie, mio signore from the Barber of Seville. TTB, T and B solos. pf. It. Eng. Text: Cesare Sterbini. GS.

597. ROUSSEL, ALBERT (1869-1937). Le Bardit des Francs. TTBB. 2 tr. C, 2 hns. F, 3 tromb. tuba, timp. perc. Fr. Text: 6th C. Book of Martyrs by Chateaubriand. DUR. (6:00). Composed 1926.

598. RUFFO, VINCENZO (-1587). Adoramus Te, ed. Robert Hufstader. TTBB. Unac. Eng. Text: asc. St. Francis of Assisi. MMC #MC78.

599. RUTTER, JOHN (1945-). Preces and Responses. TTB. OX #41.027.

600. SAINT-SAENS, CAMILLE (1835-1921). There is an impressive amount of music for men's voices by St. Saens. All are available through importation from Durand. 1. Aux Aviateurs. TTBB. Unac. Fr. Eng. 2. Aux Mineurs. TTBB. Unac. 3. Chanson D'Ancetre. TTBB. B solo. orch. 4. Chants D'Automne. TTBB. Unac. 5. Hymne au Printemps. TTBB. Unac. 6. Hymne au Travail. TTBB. Unac. 7. La Gloire, op. 131. 8. Le Matin. TTBB. Unac. 9. Les Guerriers. TTBB. Unac. 10. Les Marins de Kermor. TTBB. Unac. 11. Les Soldats de Gedeon. TTBB. Unac. 12. Les Titans. TTBB. Unac. 13. Madrigal de Psych. Men's Chorus, T solo. pf. 14. March dediée aux étudiants d'Alger. Unis, pf. men's chorus, 2 pf. 15. March Héroique. Men's chorus

and women's chorus. orch/pf. 16. Quand nous
serons devenus Gotteus (from Ascanio). TTBB.
pf. 17. Saltarelle. TTBB. Unac. 18. Serenade d'hiver. TTBB. Unac. Saltarelle is available from GS #1502.

601. SCHEIN, JOHANN (1586-1630). From Depths of Woe
       I Cry to Thee from Opella Nova. 2 ev. (TT). pf.
       Eng. Text: Luther. CON #98-1860.

602. SCHEIN. O Lord, Look Down from Heaven from
       Opella Nova. TTB. pf. Eng. Text: Luther.
       CON #98-1860.

603. SCHEIN. Studentenschmauss (Two Student Songs for
       the University of Leipzig, 1626), arr. 5 parts,
       Forbes. TTBB. Unac. Ger. GS #1057.

604. SCHMITT, FLORENT (1870-1958). De Profundis.
       TTBB. org. Lat. CUR #9561. Also Durand.

605. SCHÖNBERG, ARNOLD (1865-1951). A Survivor from
       Warsaw, op. 46. Men's unis. narrator. orch:
       3222/4331/xylophone, bells, chimes, military drums,
       B dr, timp, cymbals, tri, tamb, tam-tam, castanets,
       hp/str. Chorus in Heb. Narrator text by Schönberg
       in Eng: Fr. text, René Leibowitz, Gr. text, Mar-
       garet Peter. Pub. Bomart. (6:00). Commissioned
       by the Koussevitzky Foundation.

606. SCHÖNBERG. Sechs stücke für Männerchor (Six
       Pieces for Male Chorus), op. 35. TTBB. (1)
       Restraint (Hemung). (2) The Law (Das Gesetz).
       (3) Means of Expression (Ausdruckweise). (4) Hap-
       piness (Gluck). (5) Obligation (Landsknechte). (6)
       Yeomen (Verbundenheit). Unac. Text: Ger. Schön-
       berg. Eng. trans. D. Millar Craig and Adolph
       Weiss. BB. (14:39).

607. SCHUBERT, FRANZ (1797-1828). Also, by Schubert,
       in the collected works: Franz Schubert's Werke,
       BHL, are Terzetts for 3 men's voices (all in Vol.
       19); 1. Vorüber die stehnende Klage. TTB. Text:
       Schiller. 2. Dessen Fahne Donnersturme wallte.
       TTBB. Text: Schiller. 3. Heir umarmen sich
       getreune Gatten. TTBB. Text: Schiller. 4.
       Selig durch die Liebe. TTB. Text: Schiller.

5. Wer die steile Sternenbahn. TTB. 6. Die
Zwei Tugenwege. TTB. Text: Schiller. 7. Bar-
dengesang. TTB. Text: Ossian. 8. Mailied.
TTB. Text: Holty. 9. Trinklied in Mai. TTB.
Text: Holty. 10. Fruhlingslied. TTB. Text:
Holty. 11. Todtengraberlied. TTB. Holty. All
are in Ger. See further listings under collections.

608. SCHUBERT. Die Nacht (The Night), op. 17, no. 4,
     ed. James Erb. TTBB. Unac. Text: Ger. F. A.
     Krummacher. Eng. Alice Parker. LGGS #786.
     (2:30).

609. SCHUBERT. Der Gondelfahrer (In the Gondola), op.
     28. TTBB. pf. Text: Ger. Mayrhofer. Eng.
     Trans. HSD. AAC #103. Also LGGS #512.
     (4:00).

610. SCHUBERT. Geist der Liebe (Spirit of Lovers), op.
     11, no. 3, ed. Erb. TTBB. pf. Ger. Eng.
     Text: Matthisson. GS #774. (2:30).

611. SCHUBERT. Gesang der Geister über den Wassern
     (Song of the Spirits over the Water), op. 167. Re-
     vised, Hebert Zipper. TTTTBBBB. pf. (String
     parts on rental: 2 va. 2 vc. stb.). Ger. Text:
     Goethe. Eng. Roger Maren. EBM #41. Also
     AAC #204. Eng. Text: HSD. (10:00). Schubert
     wrote three versions of Gesang der Geister über
     den Wassern. The first was with piano (incom-
     plete); the second, four part unaccompanied; op.
     167, the third version, is for TTTTBBBB, 2 vi-
     olas, 2 cellos, and doublebass.

612. SCHUBERT. Grab und Mond (The Grave and the
     Moon), ed. Donald Plott. TTBB. Unac. Ger.
     Text: J. G. Seidl. Eng. Howard French. BR
     #DC1.

613. SCHUBERT. Hymne, op. 154 (Herr, unser Gott).
     TTBBTTBB. pf/orch: 2 ob, 2 bn, 2 tr, 3 tromb.
     Eng. Text: Lewis Novra. GS #1144. (6:00).

614. SCHUBERT. La Pastorella (The Shepherdess), ed.
     Shaw-Parker. TTBB. pf. It. Text: Goldoni.
     Eng. Alice Parker. LGGS #512.

615. SCHUBERT. Nachtgesang im Walde (Night Song in

the Forest), op. 139b, ed. Jan Meyerowitz. TTBB.
4 hns. Ger. Text: J. G. Seidl. Eng. Peter John
Stephens. BRBR #140. (6:00).

616. SCHUBERT. Salve Regina. TTBB. Unac. Text:
      attr. Herman Contractus. AAC #102.

617. SCHUBERT. Ständchen (Serenade), op. 135, ed.
      Shaw. TTBB. A solo. pf. Ger. Eng. Text:
      Franz Grillparzer. GS #521. (7:00).

618. SCHUBERT. Widerspruch (Contradiction), op. 105,
      no. 1, ed. Shaw-Parker. Ger. Text: J. G. Seidl.
      Eng. Alice Parker. LGGS #513. (3:00).

619. SCHUMAN, WILLIAM (1910-). Attention, Ladies,
      from Mail Order Madrigals. TBB. Unac. Eng.
      Text: freely adapted from the Sears, Roebuck
      1897 catalog. TP #342-40029.

620. SCHUMAN. Deo ac veritati ("Canon with Coda").
      TTB. Unac. Lat. Text: trad. Lat. Motto of
      Colgate University. TP #342-40015.

621. SCHUMAN. Four Rounds on Famous Words: Health;
      Thrift; Caution; Beauty. TTBB (SATB). Unac.
      Eng. Text: trad. TP #342-4000, 1, 2, 3. (0:30;
      1:30; 1:00; 2:15).

622. SCHUMAN. Holiday Song. TTBB (or SATB). pf.
      Eng. Text: Genevieve Taggard. GS #9866. (2:30).

623. SCHUMAN. Truth Shall Deliver. TBB. Unac. Eng.
      Text: adap. Marion Farquhar from Chaucer. GS
      #9597. (4:00).

624. SCHUMANN, ROBERT (1810-1856). Blaue Augen hat
      das Mädchen. op. 138, no. 9. TB. pf. Ger.
      Text: Geibel (from the Spanischen Liebes-Liedern).
      CFP #2392.

625. SCHUMANN. Die Rose Stand im Tau (The Rose Stood
      in the Dew), op. 65, no. 1, ed. Carl Pfatteicher.
      TTBBB. Unac. Eng. Dirk H. van der Stucken.
      Ger. Frederick Rückert. CF #CM 2109. (3:30).

626. SCHUMANN. Drei Lieder für Männerchor, op. 62.

TTBB. Unac. Ger. (1) Der Eidgenossen Nacht-
wache. Text: J. von Eichendorff. (2) Freiheit-
slied. Text: F. Rückert. (3) Schlachtgesang.
Text: F. G. Klopstock. CFP #EP 2527B.

627. SCHUMANN. Intermezzo, und schläfst du, op. 74,
no. 2 TB. pf. Ger. Text: Geibel from the
Spanischen Liebes-Liedern. CFP #2392. (1:00).

628. SCHUMANN. Jagdlieder (Five Hunting Songs), op.
137. TTBB. 4 hns. Ger. Text: Heinrich Laube.
Eng. Jean Lunn. (1) In Praise of Hunting. (2)
Be Intent. (3) Morning. (4) Daybreak. (5) Drinking Song. CFP #6614. (10:00).

629. SCHUMANN. Ritornelle, op. 65 (Canons). Unac.
Ger. Texts: Rückert. (1) Die Rose stand im Tau,
TTBBB. (3:00). (2) Lasst Lautenspiel und Becherk-
land, BB. (3) Blüt oder Schnee, TTT-TTBB. (4)
Gebt mir zu Trinken, BBB. (5) Zürne nicht des
herbstes Wind, TTBB. (6) Im Sommertagen rüste
den Schlitten, TTBB. (7) In Merres Mitten ist ein
Off'ner Laden, TTBB. CFP.

630. SCHUMANN. Sechs Lieder für vierstimmigen Männer-
chor, op. 33. TTBB. Unac. Ger. (1) Der Trau-
mende See. Text: J. Mosen. (2) Die Minnesänger.
Text: H. Heine. (3) Die Lotusblume. Text: H.
Heine. (4) Der Zecher als Doktrinar. Text: J.
Mosen. (5) Rastlose Liebe. Text: Goethe. (6)
Frühlingsglocken. Text: Reinick. CFP #EP 2527A.

631. SCHÜTZ, HEINRICH (1585-1672). Absalom, fili mi.
Bass solo with 4 tromb. (Could be men's unison
chorus). RK. (5:00).

632. SCHÜTZ. Attendite, popule meus, legem meum. B
solo. (Unis. chorus). 4 tromb. cont. Text: unknown. MRL.

633. SCHÜTZ. Eins bitte ich vom Herren (One Thing Have
I Desired) from Kleine Geistliche Konzert, ed.
Ulrich Leupold. TT. org. Eng. Ger. Text: Ps.
27:4. CON #98-1369.

634. SCHÜTZ. Erhöre mich (Give Ear, Oh Lord) from
Sacred Concert (Bk. I, no. 8), ed. Paul Boepple.

TT. org. Ger. Text: Ps. 4:1; Ps. 5:2. MMC
#MC13. (1:45).

635. SCHÜTZ. O lieber Herre Gott (O Mighty God, Our
      Lord) from Sacred Concert (Bk. I, no. 6), ed.
      Paul Boepple. TT. org. Eng. Ger. Text: Jo-
      hann Spanenburg. MMC #MC18. (3:10).

636. SCHÜTZ. Was betrübst du dich, meine Seele from
      Sacred Concert (Bk. II, no. 13), ed. Paul Boepple.
      TT(SS). cont. Various instruments possible (vn.
      ob. or fl. vc. stb. bn. ad lib.). Eng. Ger. Text:
      Ps. 42:11. MMC #MC20. (4:45).

637. SCHÜTZ. The Christmas Story: High Priests and
      Scribes, ed. Arthur Mendel. BBBB. org. (pf.)
      or 2 tromb. Ger. Eng. Text: Matt. 2:5, 6. GS
      (2:45).

638. SCHÜTZ. Christmas Story: The Wise Men from the
      East. TTB. org. (pf.) 2 vn. and bn. Eng. Ger.
      Text: Matt. 2:2. G. (2:15).

639. SEELE, THOMAS (1599-1663). Benedicam Dominum.
      TTBB. cont. Lat. Text: Ps. 33:2-3. HVS
      #FH-1, 349.

640. SEELE. Confitemini Domino. TTBB. cont. Lat.
      Text: Ps. 104:1-3. HVS #FH-1, 348.

641. SEELE. In me transierunt. TTBB. cont. Lat.
      Text: Ps. 87:17, 37:11, 18, 22. HVS #FH-1, 342.

642. SEELE. Si bona suscepimus. TTBB. cont. Lat.
      Text: Job 2:10, 1:21. HVS #FH-1, 247.

643. SERLY, TIBOR (1901-). Hymn of Nativity. TTBB.
      Unac. Eng. Text: Richard Crashaw. SOU.

644. SERLY. The Good Time Coming. TTBBB. Unac.
      Eng. Text: Charles Mackay. SOU #ME1008.

645. SESSIONS, ROGER (1895-). Mass for Unison Choir
      and Organ. Eng. EBM #77. (15:00). Composed
      1955-1956.

646. SHEPHERD, JOHN (-1563). Alleluia, confitemini

(O Give Thanks), ed. Terry. TTBB. Unac. Lat.
Eng. Text: Ps. 135:1. NOV #TM8 (GR #GCMR
1595).

647. SHEPHERD. I Give You a New Commandment, ed.
Watkins Shaw. A(T)TBB. org. ad lib. Eng.
Text: John 13:34-35. OX #18B.

648. SHEPHERD. Magnificat and Nunc dimittis, from The
First Service for men's voices, ed. C. F. Simkins.
ATTB (possible to do Alto, 8ve. higher). Unac.
Eng. Text: Luke I:46-56; Luke 2:29-32. OX #45.

649. SIBELIUS, JEAN (1865-1957). Der Ursprung des
Feuers (Tulen synty), op. 32. From the Kalevala
tale (Chapter XLVII, 4-110). TTBB. B solo. orch:
2222/4231/timp/str. (14:00). BREITKOPF. Composed in 1902. Also known as Ukko the Firemaker.

650. SIBELIUS. Metsamiehen Laulu (Forest Invocation),
op. 18, no. 5, ed. Richard D. Row. TTBB. Unac.
Eng. Text: R. Row. TOW #316. (1:30).

651. SIBELIUS. Six Part-Songs for Male Voices, op. 18.
a capella: (1) Sortunut ä äne (Kanteletar). (2)
Tervekuu (Kalevala). (3) Venematka (Kalevala).
(4) Saarilla (Kantilatar). (5) Metsamiehen Laulu
(Kivi). (6) Sydameni Laulu (Kivi). Composed 1895.

652. SIBELIUS. Natus in curas (Mortal Man Born to Sor-
row and Tribulation), op. 21, no. 2, ed. Richard
Row. TTBB. Unac. Lat. Text: Eng. trans. R.
D. Row. CF #348. (4:30). Also known as Hymne.
Composed 1897. Also, BHW #2007.

653. SIBELIUS. Song of the Athenians. op. 31A. boys
and men. 6 hns. perc. BHW. Composed 1899.

654. SIBELIUS. Sydameni Laulu (Vale of Tuoni), op. 18,
ed. Richard Row. TTBB. pf. Finnish Text: A.
Kivi. Eng. R. Row. ROW #310. (2:30).

655. SIMONS, NETTY (1913-). All Blasphemers. Text:
Benet. TTBB. Unac. ACA.

656. SMIT, LEO (1921-). Pater Noster. Male Voices.
Unac. CF (3:00).

657. SOWANDE, FELA (1905-). The Gramercy of Sleep.
      TTBB. Unac. Eng. Text: C. S. Andrews. RIC
      #NY2115.

658. SOWANDE. Words. TTBB. Unac. Eng. Text:
      C. S. Andrews. RIC #NY21114.

659. SOWERBY, LEO (1895-1968). A Liturgy of Hope.
      TTBB. S. solo. org. Eng. Text: Ps. 80. BMC
      #8065.

660. SOWERBY. Psalm 70. TTBB. org. Eng. GR
      #2995.

661. SOWERBY. Psalm 124. TTBB. org. Eng. GR
      #2986.

662. SOWERBY. Psalm 133. TTBB. org. Eng. GR
      #2982.

663. SPIES, CLAUDIO (1925-). Proverbs of Wisdom.
      TTBB. org/pf. Eng. Text: Proverbs. Com-
      missioned by Colgate University, 1964. TP #362-
      00131). (5:00).

664. SPOHR, LUDWIG (1784-1859). Blessed Are the Dead,
      ed. Arthur Ryder. TTBB. org. Eng. Text:
      paraphrase of Revelations XIV:3. BMC #807.

665. STANFORD, CHARLES (1852-1924). Songs of the Sea.
      TTBB. B. solo. pf. Eng. Text: Henry Newbolt.
      BH. (17:00). 5 mvts: (1) Drake's Drum. (2)
      Outward Bound. (3) Devon, O Devon, in Wind and
      Rain. (4) Homeward Bound. (5) The Old Superb.
      Orch: 2222/4220/timp. perc. str. BH.

666. STARER, ROBERT (1924-). Never Seek to Tell
      Thy Love. TTBB. Unac. Eng. Text: William
      Blake. SOU #ME1023. Composed 1959.

667. STARKS, HOWARD (1928-). God Wants A Man.
      TTBB. 3 tr. tromb. Eng. Text: Anon. HOPE.
      #TB200.

668. STERNE, COLIN (1921-). Three Anthems for Easter.
      TB and unison congregation. org. Eng. 1. Crave
      as Newborn Babes. Text: Peter I:2 and Ps. 80-1:5,

9-10, 12-17. 2. An Angel of the Lord. Text:
Matt. 28:2, 5, 6, and Ps. 117:1-3, 5-9. 3. Put
in Your Hand. Text: John 20-27. WL #EMP-
1595-2.

669. STEVENS, DENIS, ed. Music in Honor of St. Thomas
of Canterbury. A collection of conductus, sequences
and motets from the 12th to the 16th centuries.
NOV.

670. STEVENS, HALSEY (1908-). A Set of Three.
TTBB. Unac. 1. Weeping Cross. Text: Anon.
(2:00). 2. The Warning Moon. Text: Anon.
(2:00). 3. She That Denies Me. Text: Thomas
Heywood. (1:30).

671. STEVENS. Four Carols for Men's Voices. TBB.
Unac. (1) All This Night Shrill Cantocleer. Eng.
Text: William Austin. (2:00). (2) What Sweeter
Music. Text: Robert Heinrich. (2:00). (3) As
I Rode Out This Enderes Night. Text: Coventry
Shearman and Tailor Pageant. (1:00). (4) A Vir-
gin Most Pure. Text: Trad. (3:10). PEER #ME
1015, 6, 7, 8.

672. STEVENS. Remember Me. TBB. Text: Christina
Rossetti. MF. (2:05).

673. STOUT, ALAN (1932-). Ave Maria, op. 24c. TB.
org. ACA.

674. STOUT. Domine ne longe. Motet for Palm Sunday.
Male chorus. str, org. Lat. ACA.

675. STOUT. Inproperium, op. 68, no. 14 (motet).
TTBB. org. six str. ACA.

676. STOUT. Pater, si non potest, op. 68, no. 17. Motet for Palm Sunday. Male Chorus. Orch: tam-
tam, celesta, hp. str.

677. STRAUSS, RICHARD (1864-1949). Austria, op. 78.
TB. orch. reduced for pf. Ger. Text: Anton
Wildgans. BB.

678. STRAUSS. Schwäbische Erbschaft. TTBB. Ger.
Text: Feodor Löwe. LC #135. (2:00). Composed
1885.

679. STRAVINSKY, IGOR (1882-1971). Babel. Cantata
      from the Book of Moses I, Capital II, vs. 1-9.
      Male Chorus. narrator (male). Lat. Orch: 3
      fl. (picc.), 2 ob. 2 cl. B-flat, 2 cl. 2 bn. Bbn.
      4 hns. F, 3 tr. C, 3 tromb. timp. harp, str.
      Also available in pf. score (2 pianos). BEL. (7:00).
      Composed 1944.

680. STRAVINSKY. Le Roi des Etoiles. TTBB. orch.
      reduced for pf. Russian. Text: Constantin Bal-
      mont. Fr. Trans. Michel Calvocoressi. CFP
      #F94. (6:30).

681. STRAVINSKY. Four Russian Folksongs. TTBB(SSAA).
      Unac. Eng. Fr. Text: Russian Folk. (1) On Saint's
      Day in Chigiszkh. (2) Ovsen (Ovsen is a beneficent
      solar deity honored in Russian mythology). (3) The
      Pike. (4) Master Portly. CHES #27. (1:00;
      0:35; 1:00; 1:15). The 1954 version (post.) has 4
      horns for acc. Originally composed 1914-17.

682. STRAVINSKY. Introitus, T. S. Eliot in Memoriam.
      TB. harp, pf. 2 tam-tams (H and L), timp. (2
      players), va. stb. Text: from the Requiem Mass.
      BH. (4:00). Composed 1965.

683. STRAVINSKY. Oedipus Rex, opera-oratorio in two
      acts after Sophocles. TTBB. Solos: T., Mezzo,
      Bar., B. and speaker. Orch: 3 fl. 2 ob. Eng.
      hn. 3 cl. A, 2 bns. Bbn. 4 hns. F, 4 tr. C, 3
      tromb., tuba, timp. perc. harp, pf. str. Reduction
      for pf. by the composer. Text: adap. into Fr. by
      Jean Cocteau. trans. into Lat. J. Danieleu. Eng.
      trans. of the speaker's text by e. e. cummings.
      BH. (50:00). Composed 1926-27. Revised, 1948.

684. STRUBE, GUSTAV. Hymns to Eros, op. 19. TTBB.
      T solo. pf. Text: Ger. C. A Köhler. Eng.
      vers. George L. Osgood. BMC.

685. SUK, JOSEF (1874-1935). Ctyri Zpevy Na Slova
      Lidova Poezie Srbske, op. 18. men's chorus.
      pf. SUP.

686. SULLIVAN, SIR ARTHUR (1842-1900). Entrance and
      March of the Peers from Iolanthe. TTBB. pf.
      4 hands. Eng. Text: Gilbert. ECS #91. (5:15).

687. SULLIVAN. We Sail the Ocean Blue. TTB. pf.
Eng. Text: Gilbert. ECS #2185.

688. SULLIVAN. With Cat Like Tread (Come Friends
Who Plough the Sea) from Pirates of Penzance. TTBB. pf. Eng. Text: Gilbert. GS.
(2:30).

689. SURINACH, CARLOS (1915-). The Mission of San
Antonio: A Symphonic Canticle in five parts. TB.
Orch: 3 fl. (picc.), 3 ob. (Eng. hn.), 3 cl. B-flat
(B cl), 2 bn. contra bn. 4 hns. F, 3 tr. C, 3
tromb. tuba, timp. 3 perc. players. Celesta,
Harp, str. Lat. (1) Espada--Hallowed Trophy,
Text: trad. in honor of St. Francis of Assisi.
(2) San Juan--Song of Fauna. (3) Concepción--
Holy Womb. Text: section from Credo of the
Mass, et incarnatus est--. (4) El Alamo--Epi-
taph. (5) San Jose--Celebration. Text: Tantum
Ergo. AMP. (22:00). Commissioned by CBS,
1968.

690. SUSA, CONRAD (1935-). Lightly Come from
Chamber Music, Six Joyce Songs. TBB. ECS.

691. SWANSON, HOWARD (1909-). Nightingales. TTBB
(some div.) TB solos. Unac. Eng. Text: Robert
Bridges. MSC.

692. TALLIS, THOMAS (1505-1585). Benedictus. TTBB.
Unac. Eng. Text: Scriptural adaptation. NOV
#MT1536.

693. TALLIS. Blessed Be the Lord, ed. Walter Collins.
TTBB. Unac. org. ad lib. Eng. Text: Luke
1:68-74. AMP #NYPM--30-6.

694. TALLIS. If Ye Love Me, ed. Pantaleoni. TTBB.
Unac. Eng. Text: John 14:14-17. CON #98-1520.
(1:15).

695. TALLIS. O Lord, In Thee Is My Trust, ed. Pantaleoni. TTBB. Unac. Eng. Text: Unknown. CON
#98-1684.

696. TALLIS. Preces and Responses, ed. Simkins. ATTB/
TTBB. OX #41.020.

697. TALMADGE, CHARLES. The Junkman. TTBB. pf.
     Text: Anon. BEL #FEC. 10109.

698. TAVERNER, JOHN (1495-1545). Magnificat, trans.
     and ed. Hugh Benham. TTBB (originally for 2
     counter tenors, tenor, bass). Unac. SB #5701.

699. TAVERNER. Playnsong Mass for Four Man's Voices
     in the Dorian Mode, ed. Collins. TTBB. Unac.
     Lat. CARY.

700. TAYLOR, CLIFFORD (1923-). Balade de bon con-
     seyl from The Commencement Suite. TTB(SSA).
     Orch: 2233/4231/timp, 3 perc, pf/str. Text:
     Chaucer. ACA.

701. TCHAIKOVSKY, PETER (1840-1893). Now if Pretty
     Girls Had Wings (Tomsky's Song, 2nd Gambler's
     chorus) from The Queen of Spades. TTBB, Bar.
     solo. pf. Text: Eng. trans. Arthur Jacobs. OX
     #M11.

702. TCHEREPNIN, ALEXANDRE (1899-1977). Mass for
     Three Equal Voices, op. 102. TTB. Unac. Eng.
     CFP #66162.

703. THOMPSON, RANDALL (1899-). Quis multa gra-
     cilis from Six Odes of Horace. TBB. Unac. Lat.
     Text: Horace, Odes 1, 5. ECS #739.

704. THOMPSON. Stopping by Woods on a Snowy Evening
     from Frostiana. TTBB. pf. Eng. Text: R.
     Frost. ECS #2181-6. (3:30).

705. THOMPSON. Tarantella. TTBB. pf. Eng. Text:
     Hilaire Belloc. ECS #560. (6:00).

706. THOMPSON. The Gate of Heaven. TTBB. Unac.
     Eng. Text: Ps. 122:1; Habakkuk 2:20; Genesis
     28:17. ECS #2175.

707. THOMPSON. The Last Words of David. TTBB. pf.
     Eng. Text: II Samuel 23:3, 4. ECS #2154. (5:00).
     Arr. by the composer from the original SATB ver-
     sion. Commissioned by the Koussevitsky Founda-
     tion.

708. THOMPSON. The Pasture from Frostiana. TBB.
      pf. Eng. Text: R. Frost. ECS #2181-2. (2:15).

709. THOMPSON. The Testament of Freedom. TTBB.
      pf. or orch. Eng. Text: Thomas Jefferson. In
      4 mvts: 1. The God Who Gave Us Life. (3:15).
      2. We Have Counted the Most. (8:00). 3. We
      Fight Not for Glory. (4:45). 4. I Shall Not Die
      Without a Hope. (10:30). The work was composed
      in 1943 to celebrate the 200th birthday of Jefferson.
      It was first sung at the University of Virginia,
      which the third U.S. President founded. There
      is a complete recording by the United States Army
      Chorus, and available from the U.S. Army Band,
      Fort Myer, Virginia 22211. ECS #2118. (25:00).

710. THOMSON, VIRGIL (1896-). Agnus Dei. 3 ev.
      Unac. Lat. Text: Mass text. MMC. (2:10).

711. THOMSON. Capital Capitals. BBBB(TTBB). pf.
      Eng. Text: Gertrude Stein. Possible by solo
      quartet. Capital Capitals by Gertrude Stein, 1923,
      evokes Provence, its landscapes, food and people,
      as a conversation among the cities of Aix, Arles,
      Avignon and Les Baux, here called Capitals One,
      Two, Three and Four. It also reflects the poet's
      attachment to that sunny region, which she had
      first known as an ambulance driver in WWI. BH
      #554. (11:00). There is also a revised edition of
      1968.

712. THOMSON. Mass for Solo Voice and Unison Choir.
      pf. Lat. GS #2473.

713. THOMSON. Mass for Two Part Chorus and Percus-
      sion. Unac. Perc. player, (ad lib.). Lat. Eng.
      L. (14:00).

714. THOMSON. Missa pro Defunctis; Sanctus. TTBB.
      pf. Lat. GR.

715. TITCOMB, EVERETT (1884-1968). Behold Now,
      Praise the Lord. TTBB. pf. Eng. Text: adap.
      Ps. 134. MM #64158.

716. TITCOMB. Magnificat. 3 ev. org. Eng. Text:
      Luke I:46-56. BMC #12333.

717. TITCOMB. Missa Sancti Joannis Evangelistae.
      TTBB. Unac. Eng. Text: Mass. CF #CM444.

718. TITCOMB. The Spirit of the Lord. TTBB. Unac.
      Eng. Text: Luke 4:18-19. ABIN #APM207.

719. TOCH, ERNST (1887-1964). Geographical Fugue for
      Speaking Chorus. SATB (possible TTBB). Eng.
      Text: Toch (?). MM#60-168.

720. TOMKINS, THOMAS (1572-1656). O How Amiable
      Are Thy Dwellings, ed. Maurice Bevan. ATT(B)B
      (Can be done TTBB). opt. org. Eng. Text: Ps.
      84:1, 2. OX #38.

721. TOMKINS. The Heavens Declare the Glory of God,
      ed. Stevens. TTBB. Unac. Eng. Text: Ps.
      19:1-4. CON #98-1432.

722. TRADITIONAL Gaudeamus Igitur and Integer Vitae.
      TTBB. Unac. (Gaudeamus, Text: Poem c. 1700;
      Integer, Horatii Flecci, Lib. I Ode XXII, the music
      by Frederick F. Fleming). ECS #2321.

723. TRIMBLE, LESTER (1923-). Allas, Myn Hertes
      Queene. TTBB. Unac. or with fl. cl. bn. va.
      vc. Text: Chaucer. (5:30).

724. TRUBITT, ALLEN (1931-). The Cat in the Wood.
      TTBB. Unac. Eng. Text: Archibald MacLeish.
      RD #CB802.

725. TYE, CHRISTOPHER (1500-1573?). O Come Ye Ser-
      vents of the Lord (Laudate nomen Domini), arr.
      John Holler. TTBB. Unac. Eng. Lat. Text: Ps.
      134, free paraphrase. GR #1776. Also CON #98-
      1995.

726. VARESE, EDGARD (1883-1965). Ecuatorial. Male
      voices in unison. orch: 4 tr. 4 tromb. pf. org.
      Ondes Martenot, perc. Sp. Text: Maya Quiche,
      The Popul Vuh. RIC.

727. VAUGHAN WILLIAMS, RALPH (1872-1958). Drinking
      Song (Back and Side Go Bare) from Sir John in
      Love. TTBB. pf. Eng. Text: John Still. OX.

728. VAUGHAN WILLIAMS. Five Tudor Portraits: Epitaph

of John Jayberd of Diss. TB (some div.). pf.
Eng. Text: John Skelton. **OX.** (3:30).

729. VAUGHAN WILLIAMS. Greensleeves from a Handful
of Pleasant Delights, arr. RVW. TTBB, T solo.
Unac. **OX** #1584.

730. VAUGHAN WILLIAMS. Let Us Now Praise Famous
Men. Unis. pf. (org.). Text: Ecclesiastes.
CUR.

731. VAUGHAN WILLIAMS. Nine Carols for Male Voices.
TTBB. Unac. 1. God Rest You Merry. 2. As
Joseph Was Walking. 3. Mummers Carol. 4.
First Nowell. 5. The Lord at First. 6. The
Coventry Carol. 7. I Saw Three Ships. 8. A
Virgin Most Pure. 9. Dives and Lazarus. **OX**
#655-673.

732. VAUGHAN WILLIAMS. The Turtle Dove, arr. RVW.
TTBB, T solo. **GS** #8112.

733. VAUGHAN WILLIAMS. The New Commonwealth.
Music adapted from the Prelude to 49th Parallel.
OX.

734. VAUGHAN WILLIAMS. The Vagabond. TTBB. Unac.
Eng. Text: Robert Louis Stevenson. **BH** #5454.

735. VERDI, GIUSEPPE (1813-1901). Judgement Scene
(Act IV) from Aida. A & B solos, and men's
chorus of basses. pf. It. A. Ghislanzoni. Eng.
G. S. Laurence. **GS.**

736. VERDI. Viva Augusta from Ernani. TB. pf. It.
RIC #15150.

737. VERDI. Allegri, beviam (The Bandits Chorus) from
Ernani. TTBB. pf. It. Text: Francesco Piave.
RIC.

738. VERDI. all'erta! from Il Trovatore (Act I, sc. I,
complete). TTBB. B solo. pf. It. Text: S.
Cammarano. Eng. Text: Natalia MacFarren.
GS. (9:30).

739. VERDI. Miserere from Il Trovatore. TTBB. pf.
S & T solos. It. (includes recitative and aria;

D'amor sull'ali rosee). Text: S. Cammarano.
Eng. Natalia MacFarren. GS #6977 (Miserere
only). (3:35).

740. VERDI. Soldiers' Chorus (Orco' dadi, ma fra poco).
from Il Trovatore, (Act III). TTBB. pf. It.
Eng. Text: S. Cammarano. NOV #41. (4:00).

741. VERDI. La Vergine degl'angeli, Finale, Act II (Coro
di frati) from La Forza del Destino. Ronda, Act
III, sc. 6 from La Forza del Destino. TTBB. pf.
S. T. & B solos. It. Text: Francesco Piave.
RIC.

742. VERDI. Macbeth: Trema Banco, Act II (Coro di
sicari: Chi vi'impose unirvi a noi?). TTBB. It.
Text: Piave. RIC. (3:00).

743. VERDI. Zitti, zitti, moviamo a vendetta (Hush, Come
Quickly) from Rigoletto, arr. B. Fitzgerald. TTBB.
pf. It. Text: Francesco Piave. Eng. Bernard
Fitzgerald. FC #NY145. Also FC #NY470. It.
ed. Northcote.

744. VILLA-LOBOS, HEITOR (1887-1959). Chorus #3
(Pica-Cao). TTBB. cl. A. Sac. bn. 3 hns. 3
tromb. Text: Port.-Indian Dialect. AMP. (6:00).
Indian text, printed phonetically. A free treatment
of a Brazilian Indian Song, composed 1925.

745. VILLA-LOBOS. Mass in Honor of Saint Sebastian
(Missa Sao Sebastiao). TTB. Unac. Lat. AMP.
(24:00).

746. VILLA-LOBOS. Na Bahia Tem. TTBB. Unac.
Pert. Text: Unknown. EME. (2:00).

747. VITTORIA, TOMAS LUIS DA (1549-1611). (Also
known as Victoria). Aestimatus est, ed. Bruno
Turner. TTBB. Unac. Lat. For Holy Saturday.
CHES #17.

748. VITTORIA. Ave Maria, ed. Damrosch. TTBB.
Lat. Text: Luke 1:28. GS #6249. Also AMP;
AB; ECS #2515. (2:00).

749. VITTORIA. Domine, non sum dignus (O My God, I

Am Not Worthy), ed. Rainbow. TTBB. Unac.
Lat. Eng. Text: paraphrase of Matt. 8:8. NOV
#131.

750. VITTORIA. Jesu dulcis, ed. Archibald T. Davison.
TTBB. Unac. Lat. Text: St. Bernard. ECS #79.

751. VITTORIA. Judas, mercator pessimus, ed. D. Plott.
TTBB. Unac. Lat. Text: Unknown; possible trope
on Matt. 26:24. BR #CD#3. (1:30). Also AB.

752. VITTORIA. O sacrum convivum, ed. Nicholas Temperley. TTBB. Unac. Lat. Text: St. Thomas
Aquinas. OX #A232. (1:00). Also ECS 78.

753. VITTORIA. O vos omnes (O All Ye That Pass By),
ed. Davison. TTBB. Unac. Lat. Text: Lam.
1:12. ECS #915. (3:30). Also ed. B. Rainbow.
Lat. Eng. NOV #137 (The alto part can be sung
by 1st tenor one 8ve higher).

754. VITTORIA. Tanquam Agnus (As a Lamb), ed. Ruggero Vené. TTB(SSA). Unac. Lat. Eng. Text:
Harold Heiburg. FC #2187.

755. VITTORIA. Tenebrae factae sunt, ed. Turner.
TTBB. Unac. Lat. for Good Friday. CHES #8.

756. WAGNER, JOSEPH (1900-1974). David Jazz. TTBB.
pf. Eng. Text: Edwin Meade Robinson. ROW
#259.

757. WAGNER, RICHARD (1813-1883). Das Liebesmahl
der Apostel (Love-Feast of the Apostles). Men's
chorus and orch: 3224/4431/timp/str. BH. Good
Friday Text. There is a recording (WL. M35131)
by the New York Philharmonic, Pierre Boulez,
conductor, with the Westminster Choir.

758. WAGNER. Die Meistersinger: Act III, sc. 5.
March of the Shoemakers (Sankt Krispin lobet ihn).
TTBB; March of the Tailers (Als Nürenberg),
TTBB; March of the Bakers (Hungersnoth), TTBB.
Ger. Text: Wagner. Eng. Frederick Jameson.
GS.

759. WAGNER. The Flying Dutchman; Steersman, Leave

the Watch. TTBB. pf. Ger. Text: Wagner.
Eng. Th. Baker. GS #1164.

760. WAGNER. Lohengrin: Act III, sc. 2, In Früh'n
versammelt. TTBB-TTBB. Ger. Eng. (entire
scene very effective, would include short solos
for B and solo TTB). Text: Wagner. GS.

761. WAGNER. Parsifal: Gralsfeier (Feast of the Holy
Grail); Act I (Zum letzen Liebesmahle), arr. Rich-
ard Schmidt. TTBB. pf. 4 hands. Ger. Text:
Wagner. Eng. trans. Dr. Th. Baker. BMC.

762. WAGNER. Parsifal: Procession of Knights, arr.
McConathy. TTBB. pf. 4 hands. Ger. Text:
Wagner. Eng. McConathy. NOV.

763. WAGNER. Rienzi: Battle Hymn. TTBB. pf. Eng.
Text: Wagner. GS #1180.

764. WAGNER. Tannhauser: Pilgrims' Chorus. TTBB.
pf. Eng. Ger. Text: Wagner. GS #1164.

765. WALTON, WILLIAM (1902-). Under the Greenwood
Tree. Unis. pf. Eng. Text: As You Like It,
Shakespeare. OX #u105.

766. WASHBURN, ROBERT (1929-). Three Shakespearean
Folk Songs. TTBB. hn. F. pf. Eng. Text:
Shakespeare. 1. O Mistress Mine; Twelfth Night,
II:3. 2. Come Away, Death; Twelfth Night, II:4.
3. Sigh No More Ladies; Much Ado About Nothing,
II:3. OX #95-109. (9:30 tot.).

767. WEBBE, SAMUEL (1740-1816). Glorious Apollo.
Unac. Eng. ECS #936.

768. WEBER, CARL MARIA VON (1786-1826). Der Freischütz: Was gleicht auf Erden (Hunter's chorus).
TTBB. pf. Ger. Text: Fredrich Kind. MCA
(3:00).

769. WEBER. Schlummerlied (Song of Slumber), ed. Plott.
TTBB. Unac. Eng. Ger. Text: Anon. BR #DC2.

770. WEELKES, THOMAS (ca. 1575-1632). Let Thy Mer-
ciful Ears, O Lord, arr. S. Drummond Wolfe.

TTBB. Unac. Eng. Text: Collect, X Sun. after
Trinity, according to the Book of Common Prayer.
CON #98-1998.

771. WEELKES. Strike It Up, Tabor. TTB. Unac. Eng.
Text: Anon. ECS #537. (0:50).

772. WEIGL, VALLY (1899-). Let Down the Bars, O
Death. Text: Dickenson. TTBB. Unac. ACA.

773. WEILL, KURT (1900-1950). Das Berliner Requiem.
TBB, T.B. solos. Orch: 2 cl. 2 sax, 2 bn.
2 hns. 2 tr. 2 tromb. perc. (timp. cymbals, drum),
guitar, banjo, harmonium. UNIV. (21:00).

774. WIENHORST, RICHARD (1920-). Seven Contempor-
ary Chorale Settings for Voices. T(T)BB. Unac.
Eng. Texts: Various hymn texts. 1. Once He
Came in Blessings. 2. Now Sing We, Now Re-
joice. 3. All Praise to Thee, Eternal God. 4.
A Lamb Goes Uncomplaining Forth. 5. Jesus
Christ Lay in Death's Strong Bonds. 6. Come,
Holy Ghost. 7. All Glory Be to God on High.
CON #98-1130.

775. WILBYE, JOHN (1574-1638). Weep O Mine Eyes,
ed. Noah Greenberg. TTB. Unac. Eng. Text:
Unknown. AMP #NYPM3-1-6.

776. WILLAN, HEALEY (1880-1968). Missa Brevis.
TTBB. Unac. Eng. CON #63118.

777. WILLAN. Say Nought the Struggle. TTBB. Unac.
Eng. HARRIS.

778. WILLAN. The Three Kings. OX #41-023.

779. WILLAN. Welcome Yule. TTBB. S. solo. Unac.
Eng. Text: Anon. Eng. 15th Cent. BMI-C #3208.

780. WILLIAMS, DAVID (1887-). The Lord Is My Light
and Salvation. Male Voices in unison, fl, strb.
Eng. Text: Psalm 27:1, 4. GR #GCMR3410.

781. WILLSON, MEREDITH (1902-). The Music Man:
Three Barbershop Arrangements: 1. Lida Rose
(arr. Floyd Commet). 2. It's You (arr. Phil

Embury). 3. Sincere (arr. Embury). All TTBB.
Unac. FMC #326, 327, 329.

782. WILSON, DONALD (1927-). Madrigal. Text:
Donne. TTB. Unac. ACA.

783. WILTBERGER, AUGUST (1850-1928). Confirma hoc
Deus (O God, Preserve the Work), ed. Ruggero
Vené. TTBB. org. Eng. Text: Harold Heiberg.
FC #NY2012.

784. WILTBERGER. Terra tremuit (Trembling Seized the
Earth), ed. Vené. TTBB. org. Eng. Text: Heiberg. FC #NY2011.

785. WORD, JOSEPH. Hymn to the Night. TTBB. Unac.
Eng. Text: Longfellow. ACA.

786. WUORINEN, CHARLES (1938-). Madrigale Spirituale.
TB. 2 ob. vln. 1 and 2 vc. pf. Lat. Text: Ps.
2:1-4. ACA. (4:00).

787. WUORINEN. Super Salutem. TTBB. 3 tr. 2 hns.
3 tromb. tuba, pf. perc. Composed 1965. Pub.
Mc Gin. (7:00).

788. WUORINEN. Symphonia Sacra. TBB. 2 ob. org.
ACA.

789. WYTON, ALEC (1921-). Benedictus es Domine and
Jubilate Deo. TTB. Unac. Eng. Text: Dan. 3:52-
56. CON #98-1729; 98-1595.

790. WYTON. Mass to Honor St. John the Divine. TTBB.
congregational part. org. Eng. WL #EMO-865-8.

791. WYTON. The Law of the Lord Is Perfect. TTBB.
org/pf. Eng. Text: Ps. 19:7-10. GEM #GP304.

792. YALE UNIVERSITY. Songs of Yale, comp. and ed.
Marshall Bartholomew. 104 compositions for the
Yale Glee Club: football songs, sea chanteys, folksongs, yodels, old favorites, Yale songs. Many
are available as octavos from GS. GS #1516.

793. YANNATOS, JAMES (1929-). Buffalo Bill's. TTBB.
From Three Settings of e. e. cummings. SMP
#5646.

794. ZELTER, CARL FRIEDRICK (1758-1823). Ausgewölte
Männerchöre. Collection of 25 short pieces by a
composer who wrote much music for men's voices.
TTBB. Unac. Ger. CFP #4949. Four are published separately as Four Songs for Male Voices.
1. St. Paul. Text: I Timothy 5:23. 2. Epi-
phanias. Text: Goethe. 3. Master and Journey-
man. Text: J. K. Grubel. 2. Song of the Flea.
Text: Faust, Goethe. All are in Eng. trans. and
ed. by Carl Zytowski. TTBB. Unac. BH #5914.

795. ZIMMERMAN, HEINZ WERNER. Psalm 134. TBB,
harp. org. Eng. Text: Ps. 134. CF.

MUSIC FOR MEN'S VOICES FOUND IN
COLLECTIONS OF MUSIC

The collections are not indexed according
to title or author of the text.

ORLANDO DI LASSO. Cantiones duorum vocum
(Magnum opus I-XX), ed. Boepple. 12 Motets for 2 voices.
Unac. Lat. MP. (1) Beatus vir (Ecclesiastes 14:22). (2)
Beatus homo (Proverbs 3:13, 14). (3) Oculos non irdit
(Corinthians II:9). (4) Justus cor suum tradit (Ecclesiastes
39:6). (5) Expectatio justorum (Proverbs 10:28, 29). (6)
Qui sequitur me (John 8:12). (7) Justi tulerunt spolia (Wis-
dom 10:10, 20). (8) Sancti mei venire (Matthew 16:24).
(10) Serve bone (Matthew 25:23). (11) Fulgebant justi (Old
Breviary). (12) Sicut rosa (Old Breviary).

FRANZ LISZT. Original Music for Male Voices.
(1) Cantico del sol di San Francisco d'Assisi. Unis, B.
solo, org, and orch. (2) Mass. (3) Requiem. (4) Te
Deum (men's version). (5) Psalm 18, male chorus, orch.
(6) Psalm 116, male chorus, pf. (7) Psalm 129, male
chorus, B. solo, org. From the Collected Works, ed. Busoni,
Bartók, Raabe, de Motte. Available from Gregg, c/o JB.

FRANZ SCHUBERT. Complete Works for Men's
Voices. 4 study scores (volumes). KAL. #1060,
1061, 1062, 1097. Vol. I (#1060): (1) Nachtgesang im
Walde (Sei uns stets gegrüsst, O Nacht), op. 139b. TTBB.
2 hns. E. Ger. Text: J. G. Seidl. (6:00). (2) Hymne
(Herr, Unser Gott), op. 154. TTBB-TTBB. 2 ob. 2 cl.
C, 2 bn. 2 tr. C, 2 hn. 3 tromb. Ger. Text: Schmidl.

(6:00). (3) Gesang der Geister über den Wassern (Des
Menschen Seele gleicht dem Wasser), op. 167 (1821 version). TTTT-BBBB. va. I and II, vc. I and II, stb.
Ger. Text: Goethe. (11:00). (4) Das Dörfchen (Ich rühme
mir mein Dörfchen hier), op. 11, no. 1. TTBB. guitar
or pf. Ger. Text: Bürger. (4:00). (5) Die Nachtigall
(Bescheiden verborgen im buschichten Gang), op. 11, no. 2.
TTBB. guitar or pf. Ger. Text: Unger. (5:00). (6)
Geist der Liebe (Der Abend schleiert Flur und Hain), op. 11,
no. 3. TTTBB. guitar or pf. Ger. Text: Matthisson.
(3:00). (7) Frühlingsgesang (Schmücket die Locken), op. 16,
no. 1. TTBB. guitar or pf. Ger. Text: Von Schober.
(8) Naturgenuss (Im Abenschimmer wallt der Quell), op. 16,
no. 2. TTBB. guitar or pf. Ger. Text: Matthisson. (4:00).

SCHUBERT. Vol. II (#1061): (9) Der Gondelfahrer (Es
tanzen Mond und Sterne), op. 28. TTBB. pf. Ger. Text:
J. Mayhofer. (4:00). (10) Bootgesang, op. 52, no. 3
TTBB. pf. Ger. Text: from Walter Scott ("Fraulein vom
See") trans. Adam Strock. (2:00). (11) Zur Guten Nacht
(Horcht auf), op. 81, no. 3. TTBB. Bar. solo. pf. Ger.
Text: Rochlitz. (1:00). (12) Der Widerspruch (Wenn ich
durch Busch und Zweig), op. 105, no. 1. TTBB. pf.
Ger. Text: J. G. Seidl. (3:00). (13) Nachtelle (Die Nacht
ist heiter), op. 134. TTBB. T. solo. pf. Ger Text:
J. G. Seidl. (6:00). (14) Ständchen (Zögernd, leise), op.
135. TTBB. A. solo. pf. Ger. Text: Franz Grillparzer.
(7:00). (15) Im Gegenwärtigen Vergangenes (Ros' und Lilie).
TTBB. pf. Ger. Text: Goethe. (16) Trinklied (Freunde,
sammelt Euch). TTBB. B. solo. pf. Ger. Text: unknown.
(17) Trinklied (Auf! Jeder sei). TTBB. pf. Ger. Text:
unknown. (1:00). (18) Bergknappenlied (Hinab) ihr Brüder.
TTBB. pf. Ger. Text: unknown. (19) La Pastorella.
TTBB. pf. It. Text: Goldoni. (2:00). (20-23) Vier
Gesänge, op. 17. TTBB. Unac. Ger.: (a) Jünglingswonne.
Text: Matthisson; (B) Liebe. Text: Schiller; (C) Zum
Rundetanz. Text: Salis; (D) Die Nacht. Text: unknown.
(24-26) Drei Gesänge, op. 64. TTBB. Unac. Ger. (A)
Wehmuth. Text: H. Huttenbrenner; (B) Ewige Liebe. Text:
E. Schulze; (C) Flucht. Text: C. Lappe. (27) Monden-
schein (Des Mondes Zauber), op. 102. TTBB. T. solo.
Unac. Ger. Text: Fr. Von Schober. (28) Schlachtlied (Mit
Unserm Arm), op. 151. TTBB-TTBB. Unac. Ger. Text:
Von Klopstock. (29) Trinklied (Edit, Nonna), op. 155.
TTBB. a cap. Ger. Text: from the XIV Cent. Rittgraff's
Historische Antiquitaten. (30) Nachtmusik (Wir Stimmen),
op. 156. TTBB. Unac. Ger. Text: Sigmund von Seckendorf.

SCHUBERT. Vol. III (#1062): (31) Frühlingsgesang, op. 16 (Schmücket die Locken). (4:00). TTBB. Unac. Ger. Text: Fr. Von Schober. (32) Der Geistertanz (Die bretterne Kammer). TTBB. Unac. Ger. Text: Matthisson. (2:00). (33) Gesang der Geister über den Wassern (Des Menschen Seele), 1817 version TTBB. Unac. Ger. Text: Goethe. (34) Lied im Freien (Wie schön ist's). TTBB. Ger. Text: J. G. Salis. (4:00). (35) Sehnsucht (Nur wer die Sehnsucht). TTBBB. Unac. Ger. Text: Goethe. (36) Ruhe, Schönstes Glück der Erde. TTBB. Unac. Ger. Text: unknown. (37) Wein und Liebe (Liebchen und der Saft). TTBB. Unac. Ger. Text: Haug. (38) Der Entfernten (Wohl denk'ich). TTBB. Unac. Ger. Text: Salis. (39) Die Einsiedelei (Es rieselt). TTBB. Unac. Ger. Text: Salis. (1:00). (40) An den Frühling (Wilkommen Schöner Jüngling). TTBB. Unac. Ger. Text: Schiller. (1:00). (41) Grab und Mond (Silber blauder). TTBB. Unac. Ger. Text: Seidl. (3:00). (42) Hymne (Komm, Heil'ger Geist). TTBB-TTBB. solos. Unac. Ger. Text: A. Schmidl. (43) Wer ist gross. TTBB. 2 ob. 2 bn. 2 hn. F, 2 tr. F, timp. F, str. Ger. Text: unknown. (44) Beitrag (Birthday Song to Salieri). Ger.: (A) TTBB. Unac.; (B) TTBB. T solo. pf.; (C) Canon a tre. (45) Gesang der Geister über den Wassern (1820 version). TTTT-BBBB. 2 va. 2 vc. stb. Ger. Text: Goethe. (46) Das Dörfchen (Ich rühme mir). TTBB. Unac. Ger. Text: Bürger.

SCHUBERT. Vol. IV (#1097): (47) Gesang der Geister über den Wassern (1820 version). TTBB. pf. Ger. Text: Goethe. (48) Fischerlied (Das Fischergewerbe). TTBB. Unac. Ger. Text: Salis. (1:00). (49) Frühlingslied (Geöffnet sind des Winters Riegel). TTBBBB. Unac. Ger. Text: A. Pollak. (4:00). (50) Terzette. TTB. Unac. Ger. Text: Schiller. (A) Unendliche Freunde; (B) Hier strecket; (C) Ein jugendlicher Maienschwung; (D) Throned; (E) Majestat'sche Sonnerossa; (F) Frisch athmet; (G) Dreifach ist der Schritt.

Also, in the complete works of Schubert (Breitkopf und Härtel) the following four are for men's voices: (1) Salve Regina. TTBB. a cap. Lat. Text: Rosamunde (Schauspiele). Geistchor (In der Tiefe wohnt das Licht). TTBB. 2 hns. D, tromb.: A. T. B. Ger. Text: Von Chezy. (2) Alfonzo und Estrella (opera). Choruses for TTBB. Ger. pf. (orch.). Text: Von Schober. Act II: (A) Stille, Freunde, seht euch. B. solo; (B) Wo ist sie, was kommt ihr zu kunden. Bar. solo; (C) Die Prinzessin ist erscheinen.

S. Bar. solos. (D) Darf mich dein Kind urnarmen. S.
Bar. solos. Act III: (A) Welche Stimme. S. T. B.
solos; (B) Wehe, Wehe! Meine Vaters Scharen sch'ich.
S. T. solos; (C) Sie haben das Rufen vernommen. T.
solo. (3) Claudin Von Villa Bella. Was geht her vor.
S. T. Bar. solos, (Singspiel). 2 choruses for TTBB.
Ger. pf. (orch.). Text: Goethe. (A) Rauberlied (Mit
Mädchen sich vertragen). T. solo; (B) Finale-Deinen Wil-
len nachzugeben. T. B. solos. (&) Die Bürgschaft (opera).
Quartet: Hinter Buschen, hinterm. Lamb. TTBB. a
cap. Ger. Ardrast (opera). TTBB. pf. (orch.). Ger.
Text: John Mayrhofer. (A) Introduction: Dank dir Gotten.
T. solo; (B) Chorus und Ensemble: Dem König Heil. Bar.
solo.

Anthems for Men's Voices, Vol. II for Tenors and
Basses, ed. le Huray, Temperley, Tranchell, Willcocks.
OX. Anthems in their original languages and in translation,
from the period ca. 1450 to ca. 1800. Listed alphabetical-
ly by composer: (1) Anon. (ca. 1560). If Ye Be Risen
Again. TTBB. Unac. Eng. Text: Col. 3:1, 2. (2) Byrd,
William. Jesu nostra redemptio. TTBB. Unac. Lat.
Text: Hymn, Compline, Ascension. (3) Dunstable, John.
Veni sancte spiritus. TBB. Unac. Lat. Text: Whitsunday
Sequence, assigned to Stephen Langton. (4) Ferrabosco II,
Alphonso. Fuerunt mihi lacrime. TTBB. org. Lat.
Text: Ps. 43:3. (5) Handl, Jacob. De caelo veniet.
TTBB. Unac. Lat. Text: unknown. (6) Locke, Matthew.
Lord Rebuke Me Not. TTB. (TTB). org. Eng. Text:
Ps. 6:1-4. (7) Marcello, Benedetto. Thy Mercy Jehovah.
TTB. org. Eng. Text: Ps. 36:7-9, paraphrased, J.
Garth. (8) Marcello. To Thee, O Lord, My God. TB.
org. Eng. Text: Ps. 25:1, paraphrased. J. Garth. (9)
Palestrina, Giovanni. Ecce nunc benedicta. TTBB. (BBB).
Unac. Lat. Text: Ps. 134:1-4. (10) Palestrina. O vox
omnes. TTBB. Unac. Lat. Text: Lam. 1:12. (11) Prae-
torius, Michael. A Safe Stronghold. TTB (TTB). Unac.
Eng. Text: Luther, based on Ps. 46. (12) Praetorius.
O God, from Heaven Look Below. TTB. Unac. Eng. Text:
Luther, based on Ps. 12. (13) Purcell, Henry. Let the
Words of My Mouth. TTB. org. Eng. Text: Ps. 19:14.
(14) Purcell. Since God so Tender a Regard. TTB. org.
Eng. Text: Ps. 116. (15) Schütz, Heinrich. Jubilate Deo
in chordis. TTB. org. Eng. Lat. Text: Ps. 150:4;
Ps. 87:4. (16) Shepherd, John. Christ Rising Again.
TTBB. Unac. Eng. Text: Book of Common Prayer, 1549.
(17) Tomkins, Thomas. My Voice Shalt Thou Hear. TTBB.

Unac. Eng. Text: Ps. 51:1. (18) Tomkins. Have Mercy
Upon Me, O Lord. TTBB. Unac. Eng. Text: Ps. 5:3.
(19) Vittoria, Tomas. O Regina Caeli. TTBB. Unac.
Lat. Text: Matins, Sunday after Christmas Day.

Medieval and Renaissance Choral Music, ed. Georgia
Stevens. ev. Unac. MCR.

Sacred Chorus, Collection by Old Masters. Vol. IV
for equal voices. Unac. Lat. KAL. (1) O felix anima,
Carissimi, 3 ev.; (2) Confitemini Domino, Costantini, 3 ev.;
(3) Benedicam Dominum in omne tempore, Croce, 4 ev.;
(4) Exaudi Deus, Croce, 3 ev.; (5) Christus factus est,
Handl, 4 ev.; (6) De caelo veniet, Handl, 3 ev.; (7) Adoramus te, Lassus, 3 ev.; (8) Hodie apparuit in Israel, Lassus,
3 ev.; (9) Verbum caro, Lassus, 3 ev.; (10) Vere languores
nostros, Lotti, 3 ev.; (11) In monte oliveti, Martini, 3 ev.;
(12) O salutaris hostia, Martini, 3 ev.; (13) Tristis est anima mea, Martini, 3 ev.; (14) Jesu, salvator mundi, Mene-
gali, 3 ev.; (15) Laetamini in Domino, Nanini, 3 ev.; (16)
Christe lux vera, Palestrina, 4 ev.; (17) Confitemini Domino, Palestrina, 4 ev.; (18) Salve Regina, Palestrina, 4
ev.; (19) Sub tuum, Palestrina, 4 ev.; (20) O salutaris,
Pierre de la Rue, 4 ev.; (21) O salutaris, Pisari, 3 ev.;
(22) Adoramus te, Pitoni, 4 ev.; (23) Adoramus te, Ruffo,
4 ev.; (24) Laudate Dominum, Viadana, 4 ev.; (25) Monstra
te esse matrem, Vittoria, 3 ev.; (26) O sacrum convivium,
Vittoria, 4 ev.

Secunda Anthologia Vocalis, comp. and ed. O. Rav-
anello. Motets for 3 ev. including Anerio, Isaak, Lassus,
Lotti, Nanini, Palestrina, Pitoni, Praetorius, Tartini, Vittoria. MCR #1188.

Ten Glees, ed. Marshall Bartholomew. (Madrigals
and Airs). 3 ev. MP.

Vade Mecum, collection of motets, hymns, offertor-
ies for four male voices. Unac. Vol. II, comp. J. B.
Hoffman, JF #3485; Vol. III, comp. J. B. Hoffman, JF
#5275. Of particular interest: Vol. II: (1) Isaak: O esca
viatorum; (2) Nanini: Hodie Christus natus est; (3) Palestrina: Pie Jesu. Vol. III: (1) Anerio: Christus factus
est; (2) Casciolini: Panis angelicus; (3) Casciolini: Tenebrae factae sunt; (4) Lotti: Regina caeli; (5) Palestrina:
Tantum ergo; (6) Roselli: Adoramus te, Christe; (7) Vittoria: Popule meus.

One of the most useful collections of choral music
for men's voices is the Harvard University Glee Club Collection, in 6 vols., Archibald T. Davidson, ed.   ECS #50,
100, 1000, 1050, 1100, 1400.   Although not all are original
works for men's voices, the quality of music and editorial
scholarship make this a pioneer collection of great insight.
Many of the individual pieces are published separately by
E. C. Schirmer.   There are 32 sacred works by Anerio,
Byrd, des Prez, Gabrieli, Hassler, Lassus, Morales, Praetorius, Schütz, Sweelinck, Viadana, Vittoria; and 16 secular
pieces including madrigals by Dowland, Lassus, Marenzio,
Monteverdi, Morley, Weelkes, Wilbye.   In addition to 11
arrangements of J. S. Bach and 7 by Handel, the collection
includes Carissimi, Durante, Lotti, Pergolesi, Purcell
from the Baroque.   Although Mozart and Haydn are not included, Davison does include Gretry and Gluck who could
be considered part of the classical school.   Beethoven is
represented by 2 works.   The Romantic period together
with composers of the Russian liturgical tradition is represented by 15 compositions.   In addition, 4 operatic excerpts and 13 Gilbert and Sullivan selections are part of
the collection.   Finally, over 34 arrangements of both
familiar and non-familiar carols and folk songs round out
the survey.

In his book. Selected List of Music for Men's Voices
Knapp considers the following as original works for men's
voices (Harvard Glee Club Collection): (1) Arensky: Crys-
tal Brook. TTBB. vc. Eng. (2) Arensky: Mystic Stars.
TTBB. vc. Eng. (3) Callcott: To All You Ladies Now
on Land. TTBB. Eng. (4) Clemens non papa: Adoramus
Te. TTBB. Lat. (5) Lasso: Adoramus Te. TTBB. Lat.
(6) Lasso: Inimici autem. TTBB. Lat. (7) Lotti: Vere
languores. TTBB. Lat. (8) Morley: I Go Before My
Charmer. TTBB. Eng. (9) Sullivan: March of the Peers.
TTBB. pf. 4 hands. Eng. (10) Viadana: O Sacrum convivium. TTBB. Lat. (11) Webbe: Glorius Apollo. TTBB.
Eng.

Fifteen Anonymous Elizabethan Rounds (from a parch-
ment roll in the library of King's College, Cambridge), ed.
Jill Vlasto and William Tortolano. SB #5356.

Nineteen Liturgical Rounds, ed. Tortolano. GI
#G1600.

Anthems for Unison Choir. pf. GS #2660 (45 arrangements and original works).

A Short Mass in Canonic Style, with Rounds, Canons and Alleluias, ed. Tortolano. MCR #2870.

Five Centuries of Alleluias and Amens, comp. Hawley Ades. Shawnee Press. In 3 Vols. Men's voices: Vol. I: Van Kerle: Amen; Asola: Amen; Hassler: Amen. Vol. II: Liszt: Amen.

Friday Evening Melodies, arr. Israel Goldfarb. Unis. and 2 part. Hebrew Synagogue music. BLOCH.

The Harvard Song Book, comp. and ed. Elliot Forbes. ECS #628. (85 songs of Harvard, other colleges, traditional songs of the Harvard Glee Club and motets). Most of these arrangements are available in Octavo from ECS.

Songs of Yale, comp. and ed. Marshall Bartholomew. GS #1516.

PART II

LEARNING A SONG BY THE BARBERSHOP METHOD

Robert D. Johnson

Just What Is the Barbershop Method?

First of all, it is based on a concept that we are not a Society that sings four-part-harmony, but we are a Society that sings three parts (tenor, bari and bass) in harmony with the known melody.

Second, it is based on the belief that if a man knows or learns the melody, his eye and ear will tell him the correct note about 95% of the time at sight (first reading).

Third, it presupposes and assumes (from experience) that the basic problem in sight-reading is really caused by the words which are in the vernacular of the poet and further, are hyph-e-nat-ed to place syllables of each word in close proximity to the notes.

Therefore, we eliminate the words in the beginning and concentrate only on the notes. Thus, we become familiar with only one thing at a time. We substitute the neutral syllable "too" for words and sing "too" on every note.

One more thing please. It is essential that the group (quartet or chorus) establish Tonality first, before even starting the song:

1. Leads sound key tone.

117

    2. Basses match leads with octave below.
    3. Baritones sound 5th of Scale (sol).
    4. Tenors then sound 3rd (mi).

    (Note: This chord must be built section by sec-
    tion in this order and always be tuned to the
    lead.)

This is a chord which will "ring" and the overtone (high
key tone) should sound.

     Following the sounding of the Key chord (tonic chord)
here is the step-by-step procedure for "learning" (notice,
it is not "teaching") a new Barbershop song:

A. INTRODUCTION

    1. Everyone (bass, bari, lead, tenor and instructor)
        sings the lead part on the syllable "too."
        a) Everyone is helping the leads "learn" their
            part.
        b) Everyone is learning the lead part himself.

            (Note: Sometimes words are used on the
            "intro" because it is short; and quite often
            is the title.)

    2. Sing it (intro-lead-line) several times in firm
        unison either with the words or "too."

    3. Then each part (tenor, bari, bass) sings their
        own part (words or "too") in turn, while the
        others repeat the melody, until all three parts
        are learned.

            (Note: Here, I usually make mention of
            sharp (#), flat (♭) and natural (♮) signs
            which musicians call "accidentals." I
            prefer to think of them as "intentionals"--
            danger signs which tell the amateur that
            the next note probably isn't going to be what
            he thought it was. They are "danger sig-
            nals" and serve as a warning to the learn-
            er.)

    4. Sing intro several times until it feels good and
        sounds great.

Notice how nicely it is in tune because you take "tuning chord" each time before you sing.

B. SONG ITSELF (verse or chorus, whichever is next).

1. Everyone helps the leads "learn their part (a half of verse, a whole chorus; you must be the judge) on neutral syllable 'too'."
   a) If a mistake is made in notation or rhythm, correct it by asking the group to "put a red circle (imaginary) around such and such notes in measure so and so." This makes the learner to do the remembering for himself.) (See additional hints number 1.)

2. Sing the lead part (still with "too") several times in good unison (listen for overtones).

3. Then go to individual parts. Tenor, bari and bass all sing in turn while the rest sing the lead until all three harmony parts are learned.
   a) The man's eye and his ear will help him sing correctly. If he makes a mistake it is because his ear or his eye tells him the wrong note. Correct only on the wrong notes.
   b) Sings several times with "too."
   c) Leads must sing strong line at all times.

4. Have entire group read words rhythmically outloud in the manner of an impersonation of James Cagney, but in any case sustaining the vocal sounds.
   a) Read aloud at least twice.

5. Now you are ready to put two "familiar" things together, i.e., the words and the notes. You should be able to do this without much of a problem.

   (Note: You can now begin to give a slight indication of interpretation, but reserve the bulk of it until they are able to sing without copies. This system is for reading and learning--memorization comes with repetition.)

6. Begin all over with the next part and run it the same way.

What Has Been Accomplished?

1. Everyone knows the melody or lead part including the lead section.

2. Everyone sings in harmony with something he knows instead of singing his own part in tune with itself.

3. We are cursed with tenor, baris, and basses who have no idea of the melody--each note they sing is tuned to the last one they sang. Now they sing in harmony.

4. Everyone has "learned" it himself and was not taught. He is no longer being "trained like a seal" but is accomplishing something on his own. He is experiencing music thus making it more meaningful to himself.

5. The director or coach instead of teaching all the notes has only corrected the few wrong ones.

6. Establishing tonality each time and harmonizing with a "known" melody gives each man two points for focusing his pitch.

7. Learning it step-by-step without so much stumbling and insecurity gives each man confidence.

8. The leads will do a finer job because so many are helping them at the time they need help. Once they learn it they don't mind singing-out.

9. It will usually be in tune at all times even when in unison. You should hear chords "ringing" and hear overtones quite often.

10. You have just been "Barbershoping!"

Additional Hints

1. Singers do not sing mistakes. Every note they sing is sung because they think it is the right note (notice, I said "singers do not sing mistakes," I did not say "singers do not make mistakes"). Only the listener hears mistakes. When a mistake is heard, be sure that the singer is made aware of the mistake. In other words, the mistake becomes the problem of the

singer. Avoid the "short cut" of correcting the note
for him without involving him in the "why" and "how."
Try to determine whether the mistake is an ear or an
eye mistake and guide the singer to the discovery of
the correct sound.

2. When working on interpretation or expression, it is
suggested that all voices sing the melody again until
the desired interpretation is attained. The song (melody and words) is the important thing. Some note val-
ues may be altered to reinforce the meaning or message of the lyric. Certain key words must be stressed
to emphasize the message. An understanding and an
experience with the emotional content of the words and
melody can easily be carried over to the singing of a
part.

3. Have the singer imagine he is singing through a megaphone (the small 7 inch kind with the silver mouthpiece).
After singing several times through a phrase, while
holding the megaphone to his lips, have him sing it
again and this time put the megaphone down but leave
the silver mouthpiece in place.

This will free the tone from the throat and shape the
tone and above all, project the sound. Try it. It
works even better with real megaphones than imaginary
ones.

INTERCOLLEGIATE MUSICAL COUNCIL:
A BIT OF HISTORY

Marshall Bartholomew

The usefulness and future promise of the Intercollegiate Musical Council are due to the idea of an under-
graduate at Harvard who in 1913 felt strongly that fields
of intercollegiate competition other than sports offered a
great deal for the immediate participants and the public.
This man, Albert Pickernell, during his senior year planned
and held an intercollegiate glee club contest with Harvard,
Dartmouth, Columbia and Pennsylvania participating. Harvard, with Pickernell leading, won the contest. When he
graduated in 1914, he went to New York to work and joined
the University Glee Club of New York. This Club, founded
in 1894, is made up of men who sang in their college glee
clubs and in its membership Pickernell found the kindred
spirits to support him in his ideas. A first intercollegiate
glee club contest was held in 1914 and three additional contests were held until the entry of U.S.A. into World War I
brought them to a close. In 1916 and 1917, Princeton, Amherst and Penn State joined the original four. The contests
were resumed in 1921, eight clubs participating, New York
University having joined the group. The number grew slow-
ly. Then with funds from individuals and foundations, Harriet Steel Pickernell, an experienced concert manager, took
up her duties as Executive Secretary and later, Marshall
Bartholomew became part-time Executive Director. Through
their efforts, the program was expanded to cover the entire country.

The printed program of the "15th Annual Intercol-

legiate Glee Club Contest," held in Carnegie Hall, New
York, March 14, 1931, mentions 67 Glee Clubs competing
in 11 Regional or State Contests.   There were students
from colleges in 24 states plus a Metropolitan Region which
included Columbia, NYU, Fordham and Yale.   George Washington University participated in this 1931 Contest as winner
of the National Finals in the previous year.   Also the following regional winners: Lafayette College (Penn State Association), Washington University (Missouri Valley Association), Capitol University (Ohio State Association), Williams
College (New England Regional Association), Union College
(New York State Association).

The first National Finals Contest to be held outside
of New York City was in the Spring of 1932 when the ten
winning Clubs of the Regional Contests met at St. Louis
and Pomona College from Southern California won the Prize
Cup, with Yale 2nd and Penn State 3rd.

The climax of all previous activities of the IMC was
to have come in 1933 with an International Festival of Student Singers upon which Harriet Pinkernell and I had been
working in collaboration with the Organizing Committee of
the Chicago Centennial World's Fair.   Student Choruses
were all set to come to Chicago from 8 European countries.
The deepening economic depression in the United States and
the rapidly increasing menace of the Nazi movement in Germany and the Fascisti in Italy combined to defeat that project.

In spite of the catastrophic sequence of disappoint-
ments mentioned in this "bit of history" the IMC reached
a peak of activity in 1933-34 with a membership of 139
college glee clubs representing 19 Regional Associations.

The IMC in America remained active until World
War II made not only the former National Finals but even
the Regional Festivals impossible, although a few of the
better organized groups, such as the Southern California
and the New England Association remained active until the
outbreak of the War.

The International Student Musical Council was founded
in Munich in 1931.   Sponsored by the Intercollegiate Musical
Council and financed by Francis P. Garvan, a prominent
New York philanthropist, the moving spirits in this under-
taking were Dr. Friedrich Beck of the University of Munich

and myself. Delegates from Student Choruses of Austria,
Denmark, England, Germany, Hungary, Yugoslavia, Latvia,
Poland, Sweden, Switzerland and the United States participat-
ed. A paralyzing blow to this movement was dealt when
Friedrich Beck was murdered in the Nazi Blood Purge of
June 30, 1934. Before that tragic happening, however, the
ISMC had met in Zurich (1932) and in Copenhagen (1933).
The concert tours in the United States by the Budapest Uni-
versity Chorus (1936), Ylioppilaskunnan Laulajat of Helsinki
(1937) and Norske Studentersangforening of Oslo (1938) were
sponsored by the IMC and the ISMC.

One more meeting of the International Council was
held in Copenhagen in 1937 for the principal purpose of
laying plans for the Centennial celebration of the founding
of the Danske Studenter Sangforeningen which was to take
place during the third week of September 1939 in Copenhagen. A chorus of fifty singers from the UGC of New
York planned to join forces in Copenhagen with student
choruses from ten European countries but the Nazi army
invaded Poland September 1st of that year, the Second
World War got underway and that was the end of that well
planned international songfest.

From 1939 to 1952 the Council remained inactive.
Then Frank H. Baxter, a former President of the University
Glee Club, became President of the Council and took the
initiative to revitalize it. He devoted his efforts and resources unstintingly to this end and in 1954 the first evi-
dence of life was the highly successful Seminar at Purdue
University. Successful Seminars were held in order as
listed separately.

As to its formal organization, the Intercollegiate
Musical Council was incorporated in New York State in
1920, the incorporators, officers and directors being members of the University Glee Club, each representing his
alma mater on the Board, each keeping in touch with his
campus and speaking for it in the deliberations of the Board.
In 1957, the organization was changed so that individual
male glee clubs became members. The large Board of forty
or more elected by the University Glee Club was reduced
to seventeen, two being elected by the University Glee Club
as the Founder Member and the others being elected by the
member clubs.

When Frank H. Baxter died in 1958, his friends

and business associates established the Baxter Fund which made possible the 1961 Prize Song Contest.

The historic past was fruitful. We have a great future!

THE MALE CHORAL MUSIC OF FRANZ LISZT

James Fudge

I

In Humphrey Searle's catalogue of Liszt's one hundred and sixty-one compositions (located in Grove's Dictionary) reside 93 choral works. To many musicians this fact alone may come as a surprise, but even more surprising is the discovery that two-thirds of this genre is for male voices. Peter Raabe, early Liszt scholar and the first curator of Weimar's Liszt Museum, took the position that many of the small secular male chorus works are superior to the secular.

From both the secular and sacred works come many of the musical trademarks that form the substance of much of Liszt's creative language: tonal movement based upon roots-by-thirds; outlined chords as melodic material, especially the diminished seventh and augmented sixth chord; the employment of augmented triads at cadence points (corresponding to key words in a choral text); general use of the diminished triad; appoggiatura-like passing tones (a mark of Liszt, Wagner, Mahler and Bruckner); careful attention to the most minute dynamic fluctuations; the exercise of metric silences (for accoustical, dramatic, and textual considerations); and the wise manipulations of voice leadings.

As time progressed between 1860-85, the male chorus literature reflected an expansion of Liszt's initial

126

compositional tendencies as well as newer elements of
style. Some of the late works contain moments of tonal
obscurity, exemplified in the employment of intervals at
the major seventh and minor second, and various combinations of 4ths, 5ths and thirds.

Another discernable change occurs in the male chorus
music written after Liszt's departure from Weimar, and
upon the assumption of duties as a cleric of the Roman
Catholic church. As he himself described this music, it
had a pristine quality about it, a simplicity that was hereto-
fore absent. Perhaps the catalyst in this transformation
was the Gregorian melodies which Liszt loved for their nature and smooth melodic lines. He wove them into the
texture of his sacred male chorus pieces, either in their
actual or suggested design.

Why Liszt wrote so many secular pieces is under-
standable. The Männerchor movement was in full flower
at this time and the market to satisfy its needs must have
been lucrative. Along with many other German composers
he fared well in selling hundreds of copies to male singing
societies. As a well-traveled virtuoso he performed in the
major cities of Europe, and gradually came to know conductors and impresarios like Richard Pohl, Carl Reinecke,
Carl Riedel, Hans Bronsart, and Johann Herbeck as well
as the nationalist poets Herwegh and Fallersleben. Peter
Raabe comments upon Liszt's affinity for male-voice sonority: "He possessed until his death a justified preference
for the sound of the male chorus; in his church work we
meet male choruses up into his final life stage. This
choice also had a practical reason here, for many Catholic
churches have only male choruses at their disposal."

Some of his early secular pieces were written out
of friendship for a person or an organization. Das Deutsche
Vaterland was composed in 1841 for the King of Prussia
who, in return, decorated Liszt with the Order of Merit.
In like manner the male quartet, Trinkspruch, was dedicated to the Munich Stubenvollgesellschaft in return for a Fes-
tabend given in Liszt's honor on Oct. 31, 1843. Sebastian
Röchl describes the evening. According to Röchl, Liszt
had finished a series of concerts in and around Munich,
the final concert being for charity (a usual gesture of Liszt's).
He was thereby invited to a celebration in his honor by the
Munich Male Chorus Society. Karl Rattman, the district
leader, ushered his guest into the decorated hall where the

pianist was greeted warmly. "Now followed hours of pul-
sating life, of joyfulness and high spirits--of humor and
jokes--of raillery and pranks--of singing and toasts. Liszt
played, thanking them in stormy homage. The high point
of the evening arrived with a torchlight march. About 400
participants, each with a taper in hand, going freely through
the window laughing and singing in single file, through Unter-
and Oberganer and turning back through another window into
the hall. Since Liszt had to leave at an early hour for
Augsburg, the festivities ended at midnight, but not until
he was escorted to Der Schwartze Adler, an inn where
Goethe had once stayed. After a wait of several months
on Jan. 18, 1844 two male quartets were received and in-
scribed: 'For the gallant and enthusiastic male quartet in
the Stubenvoll, a friendly remembrance.' Weimar, Jan.
'44 FL"

     Two other male chorus pieces reflect the turmoil
of the 1840's in relation to the European industrial revolu-
tion and the general unrest of the working class. Here as
in almost every facet of his musical and non-musical life,
Liszt presents a dichotomy. He had received an early education in liberal thought through a friendship with Abbé
Felicite-Robert de Lamennais, a famous French social writ-
er and holy man, but contrary to this inclination was his
excessive desire to be accepted by all that was aristocratic.

     In fact, the first of these compositions, Arbeiterchor,
mirrors this dichotomy. Set to the poetry of Lamennais,
it was to be performed in 1848, the year of social revolu-
tion. Obviously in fear of royal disapproval, Liszt wrote
to Karl Haslinger (in charge of preparing the printing,)
"Since the circumstances of the period afford an entirely
abnormal commentary for the labor question, it would thus
appear more purposable to postpone the publication of the
Arbeiterchor. I leave the decision up to you in this matter." It is assumed Haslinger destroyed the plates.

     The second chorus depicting the struggles of the
19th century laborer is Le Forgeron (the blacksmith). It
was composed to Lamennais' poetry in Lisbon in 1845 and
was orchestrated in 1848 by Conradi (one of Liszt's several
orchestration assistants).

     Songs for special dedicatory occasions complete the
pieces of 1841-49. In 1841 three Männerchor part songs
were composed for the benefit of the Mozart Foundation:

Rheinweinlied, Studentenlied aus Goethe's Faust, the first
and second settings of Herwegh's Reiterlied.

Liszt had second thoughts about earlier details in
the Studentenlied. In a letter to Johann Herbeck, director
of the Vienna Musikverein on July 12, 1857, he thanked
the conductor for a careful reading of the piece and mentions other successful performances in Cologne, Berlin and
Paris. He also says, "When I published it 15 years ago,
I did not think much of making allowances for any possible
laxity in the intonation of singers, but today my experience
has taught me better." Care in voice leadings and a con-
cern for good intonation is characteristic of Liszt. James
Huneker, in 1911, spoke to this point, "Liszt's manner of
writing for solo and choral voices is generally practical
and effective. The voice parts are carefully written so as
to lessen the difficulties of intonation which too many far-
fetched modulations involve; and are skillfully disposed in
point of sonority."

Even during his years as a traveling virtuoso, Liszt
was preparing for his ensconcement at Weimar. He had
visited the small kingdom (the home of Goethe and Schiller)
in 1840 and had impressed the Grand-Duchess Marie (sister
of Czar Nicholas I) and her son, Karl Alexander. Karl Alexander, who was to assume the title of Grand-Duke from
his father, Carl August, prevailed upon Liszt to contract
his services to Weimar three months of every year, and
to serve as conductor and musical director to the Grand
Ducal Court. The pianist agreed, but continued to concer-
tize until 1847 when, after a series of recitals at the
Ukrainian city of Kiev, he decided to return to Weimar and
take up permanent residence. The catalyst in this turn of
events was Carolyne Sayn-Wittengenstein, daughter of a wealthy
Polish land owner and the estranged wife of an official to
the Imperial Russian Court. Liszt had met her at Kiev
and after a short courtship persuaded her to join him at
Weimar. They both arrived at the new location shortly
thereafter--he during the height of the 1848 uprisings, and
she with her daughter Princess Marie (of the former marriage) in 1849.

A work that dates from their first meeting and the
first of a long line of choral compositions for the church is
the Pater Noster for male voices. Paula Rehberg alleges
it was performed in Kiev in February of 1847 and was
heard in one of the Roman Catholic churches by the Princess.

Rehberg also claims the Pater Noster and a sketch of the
Dante Symphony convinced the Princess of Liszt's genius.

One of the larger undertakings of 1850 was the
Choruses to Herder's Unchained Prometheus. These eight
choruses (three for male voices) were intended to follow
the Overture of the work. The choruses were orchestrated
by Raff in 1850, revised and scored by Liszt in 1855, and
revised again in 1859.

At about the same point in his career Liszt was be-
coming more and more wary of public performances of his
music. As he became increasingly aware of the intonation
traps hidden within the chromatic texture of his pieces, he
began to warn conductors of the problems. To the Kapellmeister Max Seifiz at Lowenberg, he said, "I send you, according to your wish, the score Prometheus ... I think it
wiser to wait a bit. I am not in the slightest hurry to
force myself on the public and can quietly let a little more
of the nonsense about my failure in attempts at composition
to spread abroad." Liszt was, however, quite pleased with
a performance directed by Herbeck in Vienna on Feb. 26,
1860.

Two shorter pieces (sacred), Domine salvum fac regum, for tenor solo, male chorus, brass and organ, and
the Te Deum II for male chorus and organ were composed
in 1859. Liszt, in a letter to Wagner, written at Weimar
on July 10, 1857, spoke of festivities to occur in September,
and of his fear that excavations near the Goethe-Schiller
Theater might cause complications for the upcoming performances. "In that case I would have to fly to Zurich in
order to produce the Faust Symphony and my last symphonic
poem, Schiller's Ideals, at your villa. The former has been
increased by male voices singing the last eight lines of the
second part." The Faust Symphony, a Liszt masterpiece
according to Humphrey Searle, is composed on character
sketches of Gretchen, Faust and Mephistopheles. It was
completed on October 19, 1854, and the choral appendage
was added in 1857. The first performance with its addition
took place in Weimar on September 5, 1857.

At the end of Liszt's stay at Weimar there appeared,
from the publishing house of C. F. Kahnt, an edition of
twelve pieces for male voices. Entitled Für Männergesang,
these throwbacks to Das Deutsche Vaterland and Trinkspruch
had been composed variously between 1841 and 1861.

Later, on December 2, 1860, Liszt wrote directly to Kahnt sending him the seventh book of solo songs, and added the Vereinslied. He speaks of several other male chorus pieces and proposes a series of Compositions for Male Voices: "I would propose to you to bring them out in the opening numbers of a short succession of Compositions for Male Voices, and also to give them a title page.... Do not fear, dear sir, of an overproduction of this genre on my part! But by some chance one or other number of these quartets should have some spread, I should not dislike to write a couple more, either secular or sacred."

Liszt was obviously interested in exploiting the Männerchor market. On December 19 he followed the above letter with another encouraging Kahnt to get on with the publication, even suggesting a more economical method of printing the songs. He also made known the fact that another publisher, Schuberth, had been pressing him to publish these same male chorus pieces. Liszt perhaps drove home the point when he quoted a letter from his friend Louis Kohler, a pianist, teacher and composer from Königsberg, "We await your songs for male chorus, which will change these beer-brothers into half gods!"

An die Künstler (To the Artists) like the male voice compositions in the Prometheus Choruses and the final chorus from the Faust Symphony, is a significant work conceived within the '50-'61 time span of Liszt's musical writings. It is scored for solo male quartet, male chorus and orchestra. Set to the poetry of Schiller, An die Künstler was first performed at Farlsruhe in June, 1853. The performance was not successful. Raabe claims that Liszt had not yet freed himself from collaborations with others on the subject of orchestration, and that the first score, instrumented by Raff for wind ensemble, differs from the later editions of '54 and '65 for full orchestra. According to Rehberg the complement of performing forces at Karlsruhe was comprised of 260 men from the Karlsruhe, Mannheim and Darmstadt theater orchestras and choruses. The combined forces had two massed rehearsals under Liszt before the final performance. Rehberg gives us a reaction from the press, "A part of the press could not forego blustering at the new tendency of the music and also, in an immoderate manner, at the interpreters. It was stated that it was not enough for Liszt to contaminate Weimar with it, but that he was now also attempting to infect foreign cities, and besides--he understood nothing about conducting."

Liszt answered this last charge in an open letter to
Richard Pohl of Dresden in which he notes the critic's naive
compliment to the ensemble's excellence while criticizing
his conducting abilities. He states, in conclusion, that a
conductor must be something other than just an imperturba-
ble beater of time: "I think I have already said to you that
the real task of a conductor, according to my opinion, con-
sists in making himself ostensibly quasiuseless. We are
pilots, and not mechanics." A performance at Weimar on
September 5, 1857, was much more satisfying. The revised '54 version used in this performance was dedicated
to Richard Wagner.

Because of Liszt's union with Wagner and the re-
sulting Zukunst-Musik ideal, an organized opposition representing the so-called conservatism of Brahms and Schumann
became more and more vocal. The culmination of this con-
flict finally occurred at the Weimar theater of Dec. 15,
1858, during a performance of Peter Cornelius' opera The
Barber of Bagdad. An opposition led by friends of the
theater's manager, Franz Dingelstedt so disrupted the music
that Liszt refused to conduct in the theater thereafter, and
eventually resigned the post of Kapellmeister.

The composer thereupon settled in Rome near the
Vatican and began a study for minor orders in the Roman
Catholic Church. From 1862 on he became a "regular
guest at the Monastery of the Madonna del Rosario on
Monte Mario near Rome, and it was in this peaceful re-
treat that Liszt worked on most of his religious compositions." Always a loyal son of the church, he naturally
had strong beliefs about music's role in an ecclesiastic setting. In fact, after 1860, he dedicated himself to the re-
vitalizing of choral music in the church, and became a
leader in the German-speaking arm of the Roman Catholic
group for such a reform--the Cecilian Society.

But Liszt was never taken seriously by the Cecilian
movement, and his religious compositions, even in their
simplest and most refined state, were considered too the-
atrical for the church. Raabe comments upon this enigma:
"The Cecilian Society went much farther in the limitation
of what was possible in the church than did Liszt, whose
works appeared suspicious due to the boldness of their construction."

The character of his sacred male chorus music is a

modification of its more flamboyant, secular counterpart, a fact that Liszt recognized himself.   In a letter dated April 14, 1863, he said, "Everything that I have written for several years past shows something of a pristine quality which is as little to be pardoned as I am unable to alter it.   This fault, it is true, is the life-nerve of my compositions which, in fact, can only be what they are and nothing else."

In this same spirit, a genre as old as the Roman Catholic Church more and more held Liszt's musical interest and further influenced his stylistic redefinition. When selecting themes for his sacred pieces, he often chose Gregorian chant--either in a suggestive shape or in its actual form.   He was also in disagreement with the general ecclesiastic performance of chant, and strove to recapture its inherent beauty.   Raabe quotes Sambeth: "It is truly astonishing that behind this awful, consistently arbitrary, usually doggedly slow, more shouted that snug recitation of the Gregorian melody, Liszt has been able to suspect the infinite beauty which resides in those noble melodies."

The first composition considered within this period was inspired by Liszt's patron saint, St. Francis of Paula, whose likeness, painted by Steinle, hung at the Altenburg at Weimar.   The work, An den heiligen Franziskus von Paula Gebet for male chorus, harmonium or organ, three trombones, and timpani (ad lib) was composed in 1860 at the latest, revised in 1874, and published by Taborszky and Parsch in 1875.   The poetry for the setting is ascribed to Albert Apponyi.

Cantico del sol di San Francesco d'Assisi, like An den heiligen Franziskus von Paula, is a male chorus work that was also later revised (in this case, 1880-81).   It is scored for baritone solo, male chorus, orchestra, and organ, and is based on the chorale tune, In dulci jubilo.

A group of four small pieces, chronologically reaching from '63 through '65 includes two versions of Theophile Landmesser's Christmas poem, Christ ist geboren, composed in 1863.   The first is set for male chorus and organ and the second for male voices unaccompanied.   Slavino, slavno, slaveni, composed for the millenery of St. Cyril and Methodius is the third piece; the last is Crux! Hymne des marins.   Its text contains an ancient approbation presented by Pope Pius IX along with an accompanying verse

by M. Guichon de Grandpoint, Commissioner General to
the French Navy.

II

Ralph Woodward in his thesis The Large Sacred
Choral Works of Franz Liszt declares "Franz Liszt's career as a church composer was launched in 1848 with his
Männerchormesse." Although three smaller pieces for male
chorus preceded the Mass, all are miniscule by comparison,
and are like in kind to the naive Männerchor choruses of
the '40's. The 1848 Male Chorus Mass did not remain in
its original state and was revised extensively in 1853 and
1869.

The performance history of Liszt's first mass is interesting in that it spans a period of 33 years between '52
and '85, and not only traces its own history of revision,
but records a number of other events both historic and musical. The first performance of the Mass took place at the
Weimar Catholic Church in 1852 where the President of the
French Republic, later to become Napolion III, was being
honored on the occasion of his birthday. In June of 1856,
Liszt wrote to Agnes Klindworth (Madame X): "Next Wednesday I shall go to Jena where my mass is being performed
at 4 o'clock." After this second performance, the first of
several to be offered at Jena, a third occurred in Pest in
September of 1856 at the consecration of the Hermine chapel.

Johann Herbeck, Hofkapellmeister at Vienna, a noted
Austrian conductor and composer, and a friend of Liszt's
was enthralled with the Male Chorus Mass. Since his conducting duties included the Male Chorus Society of Vienna,
he was especially eager to perform the work. On January
12, 1857, Liszt cautioned against a too premature performance, and thus gives us insight to his knowledge of choral
techniques and vocal problems, primarily difficulties in intonation which are inherent to the inner voices: "Before all
else it requires the utmost certainty in intonation, which
can only be attained by practicing the parts singly (especially
the middle parts, second tenor and first bass)...." Within
the same letter Liszt indicates that instrumental support for
the voices was being contemplated as early as the above
date. Later in April of that year he spoke to Eduard Liszt
about the possibility of instruments for the Mass, but couldn't
make up his mind as to their combinations. "It would be

very agreeable to me if Herbeck, who appears to take an
interest in my work, would take the decision upon himself
accordingly to do what he thinks best, and would either keep
in the printed organ accompaniment, or write a small additional score as support to the voices."

Herbeck did accept the task, and on June 12, 1857,
Liszt wrote: "I am entirely in accord with the various
sketches you so kindly lay before me in your letter, and
only beg you, dear sir, to complete this work according
to your own best judgement, without any small considerations."

Herbeck's orchestration was used and approved by
Liszt. The composer then speaks of a possible Vienna performance: "And if the gentlemen of the Vienna Männer-
gesangverein would take the trouble to study the score pro-
perly, they might rely upon the effectiveness of the performance, provided my name is not held in abomination."

A performance of the Male Chorus Mass did take
place on October 23, 1859, for the critical Vienna public.
A sense of this is caught in Liszt's letter of Oct. 11th as
final arrangements were being discussed with Herbeck. "It
is a great pleasure to me that you are bringing about the
performance of the Mass for men's voices on the 23rd of
October, and I hope that, as you have once made your way
through it, we shall also not succeed ill. The sneaking
brood (as you well name the people) can henceforth growl
as much as they like. What does it matter to us, as long
as we remain true and faithful to our task?" Liszt con-
cludes the letter by asking Herbeck to inform him as to the
success of the performance, and since the Mass was to be
continuously refined, to send any ideas along that might better simplify and improve the declamation. In writing to
Marie on October 27 Liszt reports that Herbeck's concert
was a success, and the church where the performance took
place was full and overflowing.

Apparently the structure of the Mass did continue to
change throughout the 1850's if one is to judge from the re-
marks quoted from '57-'59 (strangely enough, the orchestrated version seems to have been abandoned after the October performance in '59, for the completely revised second
edition by Repos and Breitkopf and Härtel in 1870 was
scored for the original forces of '48 and '53).

Since 1885 it can be assumed that the Male Chorus

Mass has had an ample number of performances, especially
in Hungary, a country that has always been willing to afford its famous son a continuous hearing. The Mass, along
with the Dante Symphony, was a favorite of Wagner's who
had expected Liszt to add his name in dedication of the title
page. His disappointment was evident when he said, "Now
I learn that his Mass has been out for some time. He
knows how keen I am about the work."

                                     III

           On July 31, 1886, less than two months before his
seventy-fifth birthday, Franz Liszt died. The funeral took
place at Bayreuth on August 3, but not with the homage that
many of his friends would have wished. Liszt's British biographer, Sitwell, recounts the impressions of Walter Bache,
brother of Constance Bache and former student of Liszt's,
who attended the final ceremonies: "There was a large at-
tendance at his funeral but Walter Bache, who came from
England for the purpose, was shocked beyond measure at
the manner in which the musicians present joked together
after the ceremony. They had forgotten Liszt already on
the day of his funeral."

           For a man who had been immersed in music all of
his life, he had been denied it at his death (something
Liszt had actually preferred himself). Both at the funeral
and at the gravesite there was no music. "C.R." in an
article in the Neue Zeitschrift für Musik on September 24,
1886, admonishes the city of Bayreuth for neglecting to
sponsor a special concert and congratulates Leipzig and
Prague for doing so. Also, according to "C.R." a memorial concert sponsored by the Liszt Society took place in
Leipzig on September 9, in the Pauline Church. The Twen-
ty third Psalm for solo voice, harp and organ, Angelus for
string quartet, Liszt's Bach Fugue for organ, and the Requiem for male voices, organ, brass and timpani were given
an "outstanding performance" to a "full church." The Leipzig Lehrergesangverein "won all praise for the Requiem, a
few rehearsals qualified this talented choir, under the di-
rection of the far-seeing director-instructor, Ferdinand
Siegert, to produce this otherwise difficult work perfectly."

           Writing to Franz Brendel on June 17, 1868, Liszt
complained of not having enough time to compose, due mainly to intrusive correspondents, who bothered him and wasted

his time: "since the Coronation Mass I have in fact written
one solitary work: a Requiem for male voices with a simple organ accompaniment." He then tells Brendel that he
henceforth will be rude and aloof to such intrusions.

According to Lina Ramann, the first official Liszt
biographer, Liszt wrote the Requiem for deceased members
of his own family and for Princess Sayn-Wettgenstein, to
whom the work is dedicated and who ordered it for her own
funeral in 1887. Ramann's claim is supported in part by
a letter to Josef Dessaure on Dec. 30, 1859: "When I
have finished with some of the works which cannot be post-
poned, Daniel shall have his Requiem." On the other hand,
La Mara claims that Princess Hohenlohe heard Liszt say
the Requiem was suggested to him in 1867 on the occasion
of Emperor Maximilian's violent death in Mexico (shortly
before his tragic end the Emperor had bestowed on Liszt
the Great Cross to the Order of Guadeloupe).

Not including the psalms for male voices, there remain seven secular pieces for male chorus. The first of
the seven is also the first of three orchestral pieces, Trois
Odes Funèbres. Entitled Les Morts, this first of the odes
was composed in 1860 at the death of Liszt's son, Daniel
(although he later dedicated it to his daughter, Cosima von
Bulow), and in 1866 was augmented with male chorus and
an accompanying text by Abbé Lamennais. The poetry was
not intended to be read, and was inserted only as a "guide
for musical thought"; it has been performed in this manner,
however, according to Humphrey Searle, with moving effect,
and is thereby also given the designation, Oration for Orchestra with Male Chorus ad libitum.

Gaudeamus igitur and Das Lied der Begeisterung were
both composed for festive and patriotic occasions, and are
musically above average for their genre. Unfortunately,
manuscripts for Hungarian God and Hungarian King's Song
are unavailable. The letter, allegedly destroyed at Weimar
during World War II, is included by Humphrey Searle in
Grove's. The former was not recorded anywhere until Mar-
grit Prahacs published Liszt's Hungarian letters in 1966,
wherein Hungarian God is described.

Liszt, on March 11, 1883, wrote to Ferdinand Taborszky concerning the Hungarian King's Song: "As it is un-
certain that I shall still be alive next year, I have just
written a Hungarian King's Song ... according to an old

mode, for the opening of the New Hungarian Theater in
Radianstrasse." He included a piano score and promised
the vocal music and text in two weeks, suggesting that a
performance not take place until the opening of the theater
in 1884: "Until then we will keep quiet about it." More
than a year later the composer wrote to Baron Podmaniczky
from Weimar on September 5, 1884, and reported the completion of the work. "This past winter you asked me to
prepare a composition for the evening of the opening of the
New Royal Hungarian Theater. I have fulfilled my promise
by sending it to M. le Directeur Erkel my Hungarian King's
Song for orchestra and chorus. The execution is very easy
and lasts less than ten minutes, the sort that one can place
without embarrassment as an introduction to Erkel's St.
Stephen in the guise of a very humble patriotic homage to
His Majesty, the King.... May I extend the suggestion that
the men and women singers be dressed in Hungarian cos-
tume."

Paula Rehberg recounts that an overture had actually
been requested to precede Erkel's opera, Saint Stephen, but
that Liszt sent a national hymn set to Abranyi's poetry,
with an old revolutionary song as its basis. Because authorities thought it might offend the king, objections were
raised. The work was not performed at the opening of
the opera house on September 27, 1884, but had its first
performance instead as a special occasion there on March
25, 1885. Liszt stayed away to show his displeasure at
the original affront, and to further protest a general neglect
of his instrumental works in Budapest. The Hungarian
King's Song was later performed at Bratislava with success.

As I approached the deadline for the completion of
this study, the majority of psalm settings had not been made
available. Sometime thereafter Gregg reprint did send me
their newly published edition of Six Psalms (1864-81). Unless someone gets there first, I plan to do a study of these
pieces.

The Library of Congress did send a microfilm of
the only male chorus psalm in their possession, Psalm 129.
Composed in 1881, it is therefore among the late works and
proves that Liszt, in these late compositions, was looking
into the future.

De Profundis is, on the whole, tonally vague and seldom settles into an established key. It is divided by its

text into four sections, but the breaks in verse are nebulous in comparison to earlier Liszt choral pieces where music follows poetry exactly. Tonal abstraction in the traditional sense is perceived immediately as the organ plays the opening measures. A single-voice line is introduced in the organ's lower manual, and is made up of a series of intervals at the major seventh. Chords are shortly added in the right hand as the obscure pattern continues, and an ascending line leads to a G-flat unison entrance of the male chorus. Raabe includes Psalm 129 in his doubts about the value of the "New music" but recognizes the thrust of its avant-garde possibilities. "As in a few other of Liszt's contemporary works, the last piano pieces and songs, the Psalm 129 in the Via crucis, it is again not its musical value which compels us to listen, but rather the pointing into the future which is in none of his contemporaries so strongly present."

The psalms cover a chronological span from 1881 to 1885, and were published (with the exception of the male chorus version of Psalm 23) by Kahnt or Schuberth. Three of them, Psalm 13 (for tenor solo, mixed chorus, and orchestra), Psalm 23 (for tenor solo, harp, and organ), and Psalm 137 (for women's chorus, harp, violin, and organ) were published together by Kahnt in 1864. Liszt also hoped that Psalm 18 (for male chorus and orchestra) might be included but it was not. He discussed the possibility in a letter to Franz Brendel on November 11, 1863. Kahnt had made a complimentary reference to the psalms in an article in the Neue Zeitschrift für Musik (Kahnt had replaced Schumann as editor after the latter's death). Liszt appreciated the review and hoped that their promised publication by Kahnt would shortly materialize. "His reference to my psalm leads me to wish that I might soon see the four psalms published in score (they are diverse, both as regards feeling and musical form). Kahnt's willingness to publish them is, therefore, welcome news to me, and I beg he will give me a proof of his goodwill by kindly having them ready for next Easter's sale."

The psalms apparently were performed often in the German-speaking countries of Europe and in Hungary during Liszt's lifetime. The composer, always with an eye for wider circulation of his works, had them translated into French (as well as some of his Lieder) by a Monsieur Lagye. He seemed pleased with Lagye's efforts and, in a letter to Mme. Tradieu on September 12, 1882, hoped for

success in both France and Belgium. "His translations appear to me really excellent, very carefully made and pro-
sodically well suited to the music. I only regret to have
to give him so much trouble, but I hope that in the end he
will be satisfied with me. He shall have the second copy
of my Lieder; if he succeeds as well in putting them into
French as he has done with the three Psalms, they may
with advantage make their way in Belgium and still farther."

SELECTED MASS SETTINGS BY TWENTIETH
CENTURY COMPOSERS

(FROM THE MASS AND THE TWENTIETH
CENTURY COMPOSER)

William Tortolano

ERNST KRENEK

The irrepressible fecundity of Ernst Krenek (b. 1900)
is not only apparent from his opus numbers (presently over
120) but from his prolific use of various structural forms.
A severely intellectual composer, Krenek is no longer interested in reaching the big public. Bristling with com-
plexities and making no concessions, his is an expression
of certain advanced techniques in Twentieth Century musical
craftsmanship.

Krenek, like many 12 Tone Technicians (in a letter
to the author from Mr. Krenek about his Mass, he calls
the Mass "related to dedacaphony"), has written a numer-
ically small proportion of sacred compositions. His four
sacred compositions are the exemplification of 12 Tone
Technique, but functionalized for textural and practical usage
of voices. These are:

1. Proprium Missae in Festo Innocentium, 1940
2. Lamentation Jeremiae, Secundum Breviorum
   Sacro-sanctae Ecclesiae Romanae, 1940
3. In Paradisum, 1940
4. Missa Duodecim Tonorum, 1957

141

The Missa Duodecim Tonorum is, as its title indicates,
a work in the Twelve Tone Technique, and it may well be the
first important Mass so written. It is a sober intellectually-
conceived, highly musical composition. It is "not the system,
in itself, that matters, but what it can express and how through
the system, the music can develop into a thing of beauty."

One has the general impression that the Mass ex-
emplifies introspective quiet and conservatism. The practical usage of teaching a tone row and showing its variations
to a nonprofessional choir makes this Mass easy to teach.
The range and general voice lines of his Three Part Mass
are imposed over a quasi-independent organ accompaniment
that is aware of voice leading and cuing.

It was designed so as to be accessible and acceptable
to the parish choir. It is part of a series of six commissioned Masses by contemporary composers called Connois-
seur's Catalog published by the Gregorian Institute of America. All the Masses were intended as liturgically functional.
The introduction to this catalog makes a fervent plea for
new musical settings of the Mass:

> Because of the natural conservatism and function-
> alism of the Church's artistic viewpoint, works of
> more traditional flavor have found more extensive
> acceptance by our choirs and congregations. On
> the other hand, the church musician deserves an
> opportunity to hear and perform new music.

This work possesses a true liturgical character with
a true and vivid reflection of the texts set to music. Mr.
Krenek does not write for "community singing" but for musicians who want pure musical ideals.

This is not a Mass to be learned in one easy lesson.
It is far removed from the traditional Romantic harmony
we hear in our churches. There are many factors that
make it accessible. The voice ranges are comfortable.
Melodic skips are small, the largest being an infrequent
sixth. Melodic progressions within phrases are diatonic.
The accompaniment is simple.

ROY HARRIS

One finds the Mass for Male Voices and Organ by
Roy Harris a unique enigma.

A major work, by a major American composer, it has never been published. No description or critique can be found, except the initial reviews it received the evening of its world premiere at a major contemporary musical festival. No reference is made of it in any way whatsoever in Catholic books or journals.

Perhaps its non-musical controversy stems from the premiere it received at the Columbia University Festival in New York on May 13, 1948. "Composed for the Catholic people of America," it was "originally intended for performance at St. Patrick's Cathedral in New York, but was called off by the Cathedral officials in protest against Harris' interview published in the New York Times of 15 February, 1948, headlined--'Composing for cash, Harris proves composer can get paid for work' containing an oblique reference to a Mass scheduled to be performed at St. Patrick's Cathedral, implying the work, too, was written for cash, which it wasn't."

One is amazed that such a conclusion was arrived at. There simply is no reference to any unethical practice on the part of Harris. But even if he had been commissioned to write a Mass (for cash), this is an ethical practice long enjoyed by composers. The Renaissance was full of musical patrons who commissioned composers.

The music itself is not controversial. It is completely liturgical in its use of words, length and style.

The Credo, the downfall of many composers, is perhaps the weakest part of this Mass. The rest of the work is contrapuntally conceived with a judicious accompaniment that gives support to crucial places.

Harris (1898-1979) captured the imagination of Americans in the Thirties as no other composer had. He was frequently performed and greatly admired. This was a decade of intense American nationalism that produced music by Roy Harris, Aaron Copland, and George Gershwin that immediately appealed to the average man. The Second World War and its aftermath brought a new era that found the music of the Thirties old-fashioned and passe. Roy Harris and his musical star went into eclipse, never to emerge again as a potent personality.

The Mass contains no reference to any Americana,

nor to any other type of outside influence. It is simply a
well-wrought setting of the Mass that deserves to be heard.

LOU HARRISON

Lou Harrison (Portland, Oregon, 1917-) "has been
influenced variously by Neo-Classicism, by Schönberg, by
Sixteenth Century counterpoint, and by the exotic sounds of
Hindu and Balinese music." Harrison studied with Schönberg for six months, who then dismissed him with the ad-
vice that henceforth his only teacher should be Mozart.
The major event in his creative life has been his redis-
covery of the interval. Early in his career he investigated
microtones. Although many of his works are in the 12
tone technique "he accepted it primarily in the way Schönberg intended, as a method of releasing his music from the
implications of key harmony."

It seems surprising that a composer of diverse compositional interests should compose an articulate Mass to
unison or octave singing. Introduced in New York in 1954,
the Mass to the Glory of God occupied the composer at various times from 1941 to 1952. It is scored for male and
female voices, trumpet, harp and strings and dedicated to
St. Anthony. It is distinguished by its restraint, the individual characterization of each section without recourse to
drama, and the freedom of the musical line. It is truly
an extraordinary achievement to write an extended work for
unison chorus and the lack of contrapuntal involvement.
"The melodies are inspired by a simple kind of plainsong
which the Indians sang in Spanish California and Mexico.
There is no declaration that they were taken from any kind
of extant themes." Except for a short baritone sacred solo,
the only religious composition from his pen is the Mass.

Living in a period of post-dodecaphony, the Mass is
a pinnacle of tone-emancipation. "Like music composed before the 300 year harmonic era it has no key harmony, no
modulation: it is composed in euphony instead of disson-
ance. It lacks all shocks to which the shock-eared listener
is accustomed."

A slow but decisive composer, Harrison manifests in
this Mass his involvement with rhythm. One feels an overall subtlizing of rhythm. The limpid modal vocal lines
bear a close resemblance to flexible Gregorian melodies.

Highly undramatic, cast in a concise mold and musically
interesting, it is a worthy addition to our literature.

JEAN LANGLAIS

Deeply rooted in the French tradition of his teachers,
Tournemire, Paul Dukas, André Marchal and the association
and encouragement of Olivier Messiaen and Marcel Dupré,
the blind Jean Langlais catapulted to fame when he became
successor at St. Clotilde. This coveted post was once held
by Cesar Franck. The unmistakable feature of his five
Masses to date, is an alignment with tradition.

Langlais is one of the most difficult composers to
make generalizations about. The separate movements of
the Mass somehow make a unified whole by "a style that
combines the traits of Impressionism with a stark modal
technique," and the skillful use of contemporary techniques
and compositional devices. These compositional devices include an abundant use of Gregorian themes (e.g., Mass in
Ancient Style) and Renaissance ideals (e.g., Missa Salve
Regina). Langlais also inherits the modern French predi-
lection for imitative writing. These are general observa-
tions. Each Mass section has distinct characteristics, and
the overall combination of sections has a common general
feature. Here is a list of the five Masses:

1. Messe Solennelle for Chorus of Mixed
   Voices and Organ, 1952.

This Mass occupied the composer for 12 years and
was his first Mass setting. Half the Mass is inspired by
Gregorian Chant and half uses original themes.

The Gloria is inspired by the Gregorian Gloria XIII.
The remainder of the composition (no Credo) abandons chant
motifs in favor of original themes.

2. Missa in Simpliciatate, for single voice or
   unison chorus and organ, was dedicated to
   Jeannine Collard, French mezzo-soprano.

Outside of Gregorian Masses and "peoples" unison
Masses, there are very few Masses for solo voices. The
deceptively simple language of this Mass is a mystic union
of human voice and organ accompaniment through its inti-
macy of expression. The recurring motifs are original.

3. Mass in Ancient Style, for mixed voices, a
    cappela, 1952.

This Mass was written at a publisher's request that
he compose a Mass "that might readily fall within the tech-
nical grasp of parish choirs, in a more diatonic style than
Messe Solennelle."

Fortunately, this Mass will never clutter advertising
space and sales counters as a "short and easy" Mass in
the company of the enormous number of second-rate settings.
It is in a class by itself.

It draws its inspiration from the Renaissance, and
demands hard study to prepare.

4. Missa Salve Regina, for men's three part
    chorus, people's unison chorus, 3 trumpets,
    5 trombones and organs, 1954.

Perhaps the most remarkable setting, it profusely
uses the Gregorian "Salve Regina" as a free basis.   The
chapter on melody will show in detail his success with this
melody.   We quote from M. Langlais:

> The composer has sought in this work to recreate
> the poetic as well as the religious environment of
> the Middle Ages.   He has therefore purposely
> drawn his inspiration from such sources as Pero-
> tin, Guillaume de Machaut and Dufay.   The Main
> lines of the admirable hymn Salve Regina in the
> first mode form the free basis of the work.   This
> Mass, destined in an initial hearing under the
> vaults of Notre Dame, was conceived as a vast
> sonorous fresco of a decorative character befitting
> the grandoise edifice where it was first given on
> Christmas night 1954.

5. Missa Misericordiae Domini, for soprano,
    tenor, bass, chorus and organ, 1959.

This Mass is part of a series of commissioned Masses by the Gregorian Institute of America.

TWENTIETH CENTURY MALE CHORAL MUSIC
SUITABLE FOR PROTESTANT WORSHIP
(from a doctoral dissertation, pp. 24-27 and 52-56)

John William Lundberg

In a real sense the beginnings of the Renaissance
marked the beginning of male choral music. All the in-
gredients were present: part writing; more than one singer;
and male singers. While it was true that parts were written for what we would call soprano and alto, it would not
be accurate to say that Renaissance choral music was the
same as the modern day SATB arrangement. The chief
difference lay in the alto part which was often written too
low to accommodate female voices. In his exhaustive treatment of Renaissance choral music, Herbert R. Pankratz
concluded that the construction of the alto part was such
that it must have been intended to be sung by men rather
than women. Further he pointed up the problems that re-
sult from attempts to re-align parts for mixed choir music
that was originally written for Renaissance voicing. He
found that the range of the alto part was not much higher
than the tenor and often as low or nearly as low. Often
the line dropped to D, and sometimes C, notes completely
out of the range of the female alto voice. In order to accommodate the female voice, a transposition to a higher
key became a necessity, but this moved the tenor so high
that most tenors found it too taxing to negotiate. The same
dilemma persisted in the bass part, with the line rising
above middle C on many occasions.

As in previous periods, participation in vocal en-

sembles was limited to men, or men and boys. Willi Apel
notes that even in the secular music of the time, there is
nothing that would suggest participation on the part of wom-
en either in church, in the courts, or in civic affairs. He
cites one exception: a liturgical drama of the Resurrection
(c. 1100) involving dialogue between the angel and the women
at the tomb.

     Pankratz observes that in Germany similar restric-
tions were imposed on women in secular activities as well.
There, however, the situation depended on social conditions
rather than on some basic concept of appropriateness.

          If there was an a priori principle concerning the
          performance of choral parts, in church, town, and
          school situations ... it was this: that girls or
          women were not to be found amongst the members
          of these groups. This conclusion is supported by
          all historical knowledge concerning such organiza-
          tions (particularly as seen in membership rosters)
          as well as knowledge of the social structure of
          the times.

     Because women were banned from participation in
the services of the church, the upper parts of choral music
were of necessity assigned to men singing falsetto, to castrati, or to boys. During the Middle Ages falsetto had been
used in the highest parts, but as early as the thirteenth
century adult males began to be supplanted by boy sopranos.
The use of boy sopranos became very popular during the
fifteenth century. Adult males, however, were used on the
alto part, falsetto being used to negotiate the higher notes.

     It is well known that the gathering of male voices
together in something akin to SATB voicing did not emerge
until c. 1500, in the writings of Ockeghem, Obrecht, des
Prez, and others. To the casual observer it might appear
that the sound of Renaissance music was similar to the
familiar SATB voicing of our day, but the use of men and
boys produced significant differences in performance. On
the one hand, boy sopranos sang with a more flute-like
sound than the typical female soprano, lighter in texture
and more devoid of vibrato. Then, too, the alto part, sung
by men in the upper part of their range, produced a heavier,
more intense sound than that of female altos singing in a
lower, more comfortable range.

     Many musical clubs appeared during the period of the

Commonwealth.   There were also clubs at St. John's College, Oxford and Cambridge.   Samuel Pepys (1664) mentions his going to a "Musique Meeting."   From his Musical
Companion (1701), it appears that the music publisher Henry Playford was active in promoting Catch Clubs on a national scale:

> And that he [the publisher] may be beneficial to
> the publick in forwarding a commendable socie-
> ty ... he has prevailed with his acquaintance and
> others in this city to enter into several clubs
> weekly, at taverns of convenient distance from
> each other, having each a particular master of
> musick belonging to the society established in it,
> who may instruct those, if desir'd, who shall be
> unskilled, in bearing a part in the several catches
> contained in this book, as well as others....   In
> order to this he has provided several articles to
> be drawn, printed, and put in handsome frames,
> to be put up in each respective room the societies
> shall meet in, and be observed as so many stand-
> ing rules, which each respective society is to go
> by; and he questions not but the several cities,
> towns, corporations, etc., in the kingdom of Great
> Britain and Ireland, as well as foreign plantations,
> will follow the example of the well-wishers to
> vocal and instrumental musick in this famous city,
> by establishing such weekly meetings as may ren-
> der his undertaking as generally received as it is
> useful.   And if any body or bodies of gentlemen
> are willing to enter into or compose such socie-
> ties, they may send to him, where they may be
> furnished with books and articles.

Men's vocal ensembles began to flourish in England
in the latter part of the eighteenth century with the formation of "Glee Clubs," and "Catch Clubs" that met regularly
to sing glees, rounds, and catches.   The Noblemen's and
Gentlemen's Catch Club was organized in 1761, and from
its membership came one of the most important publications
of the period, the Collection of Catches, Canons, and Glees,
compiled and edited by Thomas Warren (d. 1794), who was
the secretary of the Club.   The publication was issued an-
nually and eventually included 652 selections.

Other clubs included the Canterbury Catch Club (1779),
the London Club, Concertores Sodales (1798), the Anacreon-
tic Society (1776), --Haydn once visited this club--and the

Catch Club of Calcutta. It is interesting to note that the
famous Huddersfield Choral Society began as a club (1836),
and continued in this form for several years.

The glee was distinctively homophonic, in a simple
note-against-note, and markedly sectional. The glee was
independent of any instrumental accompaniment whatever.
Although some compositions with accompaniment were called
glees, this, according to John Hullah, was a misnomer and
would be more appropriately called accompanied trios, quartets, and choruses.

The catch differed from the glee, being more closely
related to the round. The term implied that the singer
"catch up," much in the same manner as the Italian caccia.
Written in the style of a round, the interweaving of the
texts often produced ludicrously humorous puns. For example, J. W. Callcott's catch concerned the appearance in
the same year of Hawkin's and Burney's Histories of Music
(1776). The text read, "Have you Sir John Hawkin's History? Some folks think it's quite a mystery," which was
followed by, "Burney's history I like best." When sung
together, one voice sang, "Sir John Hawkins," while the
entrance of the second voice confused the text to sound like,
"Burn 'is history." The inference of verbal humor was not
necessarily a distinguishing feature at an earlier period,
when the term applied to any round or short composition of
that nature.

Many of the important composers of the day also
wrote glees (e.g., Purcell, Arne, Boyce). Other composers who are remembered for their contribution to this
form of composition include: Attwood, Battishill, Cooke,
Danby, Hindle, Samuel Webbe, John Stafford Smith, Stephen
Paxton, William Paxton, Lord Mornington, Richard Stevens,
J. W. Callcott, Reginald Spofforth, and William Horsley.

The contribution of Samuel Webbe (1740-1816) was
significant. He was considered to be the founder of the
school of the glee, and his Glorious Apollo was the most
famous glee of all. Written for the Glee Club (founded,
1783), it was regularly sung at the beginning of each club
meeting. The first time through it was sung by three solo
voices, and on the repeat the entire group joined in.

The contribution of Barber Shop music to the develop-
ment of the male ensemble is often overlooked. Percy
Scholes acknowledges this:

> The barbers are rarely or never mentioned in
> books of musical reference. They are included
> in the present one ... because they really played
> a part in musical life and for a pretty extended
> period--and ... not only in Britain.

The barber shop served as a haunt for music during the sixteenth, seventeenth, and early eighteenth centuries. While waiting for haircuts, blood letting, or tooth drawing, customers would engage in music making, with instrumental music assuming a prominent role. The cittern was especially popular.

TITLE IX AND THE MEN'S GLEE CLUB

Robert F. Grose

In discussion and analysis of Title IX concerning
non-discrimination on the basis of sex under Federally as-
sisted education programs and activities from the Office
of Education, there is found mentioned in Section 43 of the
introductory material, Federal Register, Volume 40, No.
108, Wednesday, June 4, 1975, as follows:

> Paragraph 86.34. (a) is redesignated as Section
> 86.34 and is amended further by adding six para-
> graphs containing language: (f) Allowing recipients
> to offer a chorus or choruses composed of mem-
> bers of one sex if those choruses are based on
> vocal range or quality....

The actual text as the final regulations are published,
therefore, reads as follows:

> Section 86.34. Access to course offerings.
>
> A recipient shall not provide any course or other-
> wise carry out any of its education program or
> activity separately on the basis of sex, or require
> or refuse participation therein by any of its stu-
> dents on such basis, including health, physical
> education, industrial, business, vocation, techni-
> cal, home economics, music, and adult education
> courses....
>
> (f) Recipients may make requirements based on vocal

152

> range or quality which may result in a chorus
> or choruses of one or predominantly one sex....

This does seem to me to be the basic position in
implementing the spirit of the law as reflected in the opening statement under Title IX.

> No person in the United States shall, on the basis
> of sex, be excluded from participation in, be de-
> nied the benefits of, or be subjected to discrim-
> ination under any education program or activity
> receiving Federal financial assistance.

I would feel fairly confident that the above Section
(86.34) would clearly hold up as consonant with Title IX
regulations and its spirit. I do not know of any amend-
ments introduced to modify this position. It would suggest,
therefore, that the labels of men's and women's choruses
or groups be eliminated, although there would be no reason
not to continue the study and presentation of musical literature for groups with certain vocal ranges. The text would
simply be whether there was discrimination based on sex
as against the voice quality and range of the individual
whose voice is in question.

Moreover, it would be expected that musical groups
of different vocal ranges would not, in and of themselves,
be discriminated against or favored simply due to the pres-
ence of men and women. The treatment of students is
meant to be without discrimination on the basis of sex except for certain clearly specified exceptions.

Perhaps useful would be these basic questions found
on page 64 of "Implementing Institutional Self-Evaluation--
Complying with Title IX" (U.S. Department of Health, Education, and Welfare, Office of Education):

> Are all extracurricular activities conducted, oper-
> ated, sponsored or supported by the education
> agency or school operated without differentiation
> on the basis of sex?....
>
> Is participation in all extracurricular activities
> open equally to both females and males?....
>
> Are male and female participants treated equally
> in all extracurricular activities?....

It would appear that even with the use of the concept of "vocal range" it is expected that equivalent oppor-
tunities will be made available for both women and men
vocalists.

BIBLIOGRAPHY

A CHECKLIST OF TWENTIETH-CENTURY CHORAL MUSIC
FOR MALE VOICES by Kenneth Roberts. Pub. by Information Coordinators, Inc, 1435 Randolph St., De-
troit 48226, 1970. A good guide to contemporary
music.

CATALOG OF THE DRINKER LIBRARY OF CHORAL MUSIC
AND THE AMERICAN CHORAL FOUNDATION LIBRARY.
The Free Library of Philadelphia, Logan Square, Philadelphia, Pennsylvania 19103. Helpful notes about
most of the Bach Cantatas and selected small catalog
of men's choral music. 1971.

CATALOGUE OF CANADIAN CHORAL MUSIC (CATALOGUE
DE MUSIQUE CHORALE CANADIENNE) ed. by John
Peter Lee Roberts. Pub. by the Canadian Music Cen-
tre, 1263 Bay St., Toronto, Ontario M5R 2C1, Canada.
1978.

CHORAL MUSIC IN PRINT, VOL. I: SACRED CHORAL
MUSIC, ed. by Thomas Nardone, James Nye, Mark
Resnick. Pub. Musicdata. Inc., Philadelphia. 1974.

CHORAL MUSIC IN PRINT, VOL. II: SECULAR CHORAL
MUSIC, ed. by Thomas Nardone, James Nye, Mark
Resnick. Pub. Music data, Inc., Philadelphia. 1974.

CHORAL MUSIC IN PRINT, 1976 SUPPLEMENT, ed. Thomas Nardone. Pub. Musicdata, Inc., Philadelphia, 1976.

HANDBUCH DER CHORMUSIC, BAND I (VOL. I), 1953.
   by Erich Valentin.   Pub. by Gustav Bosse Verlag,
   Regensburg.   Also Band II (VOL. II), 1958.

KNAPP, J. MERRILL: SELECTED LIST OF MUSIC FOR
   MEN'S VOICES.   Princeton, N.J.:   Princeton University Press, 1952.   An excellent primary source and a
   "standard" reference source.   The book is out of print
   and many titles are no longer available.   Knapp includes
   many pieces arranged for male voices.

LOCKE, ARTHUR WARE and FASSETT, CHARLES: SE-
   LECTED LIST OF CHORUSES FOR WOMEN'S VOICE.
   1964.   Smith College, Northampton, Mass.

MUSIC OF THE TWENTIETH CENTURY.   Catalog of Composers Recordings, Inc., 170 West 74th St., New York,
   N.Y.   10023.   (212-873-1250).

THE ALEXANDER BROUDE, INC.   COMPREHENSIVE GUIDE
   TO ORCHESTRAL MUSIC (2 catalogue).   Compiled and
   edited by James Laughlin.   Pub. Alexander Broude,
   Ind.   116pp.

TWENTIETH-CENTURY MALE CHORAL MUSIC SUITABLE
   FOR PROTESTANT WORSHIP by John Lundberg.   Pub.
   University Microfilms, Ann Arbor.   1974.

MASS AND THE TWENTIETH-CENTURY COMPOSER, THE
   by William Tortolano.   Pub. University Microfilms,
   Ann Arbor.   1964.

INDEX OF AUTHORS
AND SOURCES OF TEXTS

Gloria; Mass Text - Gretchaninoff, 294
Gloria; Mass Text - Mathias, 460
Gloria; Mass Text - Power, 574
Goethe, Johann Wolfgang von (1749-1832) - Beethoven, 80
Goethe - Brahms, 112
Goethe - Liszt, 422
Goethe - Schubert, 611
Goethe - Schumann, 630
Goethe - Zelter, 794
Goldoni, Carlo (1707-1793) - Schubert, 614
Goliard Lyrics, Medieval - Malipiero, 446
Goodman, Paul (1911-) - Rorem, 590
Gosse, Edmund (1849-1928) - Elgar, 248
Gower, John - Bennett, 66
Grainger, Percy (1882-1961) - Grieg, 300
Gratias agimus tibi; Mass Text - Hassler, 321
Graves, Robert (Alfred Perceval) (1846-1931) - Adler, 3
Greek, Anon. - Benjamin, 65
Greek, 3rd Cent. - Bourgeois, 108
Greek - Elgar, 248
Grillparzer, Franz (1791-1872) - Schubert, 617
Grübel, J. K. - Zelter, 794
Gulding, Arthur - Bennett, 66

Habakkuk 2:20 - Thompson, 706
Halevy, Ludovic (1834-1908) - Bizet, 101
Halevy - Offenbach, 522
Hall, Robert A. - Mendelssohn, 474
Harding, Washburn - Hadley, 303
Hardinge, W. M. - Elgar, 248
Hart, Henry - Korte, 389, 393
Harte, Bret (1836-1902) - Elgar, 249
Hebrew Liturgy - Blow, 107
Hebrew Liturgy - Kahn, 366
Hebrew Liturgy - Lewandowski, 419, 420
Heiburg, Harold - Aichinger, 5
Heiburg - Vittoria, 754
Heiburg - Wiltberger, 783, 784
Heine, Heinrich (1797-1856) - Schumann, 630
Heinrich, Robert - Stevens, 671
Herrick, Robert (1591-1674) - Adler, 1
Herrick - Bacon, 38
Herrick - Berkeley, 78
Herrick - Hastings, 324
Hunt, Leigh - Mechem, 468
Heywood, Thomas - Stevens, 670
Hoffman, R. S. - Delius, 213

Pantaleoni - Praetorius, 575
Parker, Alice (1925-) - Schubert, 608, 614, 618
Pentecost Texts - Felciano, 259
Peter 1:2 - Sterne, 668
Peter, Margaret - Schönberg, 605
Petofi, Sàndor (1823-1849) - Kodály, 379
Petran, Franz - Mozart, 503
Philippians 4:4-7 - Causton, 150
Philipott (1641-) - Berger, 74
Piave, Francesco (1810-1876) - Verdi, 736, 737, 741, 742,
    743
Picander (Christian Friedrich Henrici) (1700-1764) - Bach,
    33, 35
Pitfield, Thomas (1903-) - Pitfield, 558, 560
Pleni Sunt Caeli, Mass Text - Des Prez, 219
Plomer, William (1903-) - Britten, 114
Plutzik, Hyam - Barlow, 46
Prammersberger, Max - Bruckner, 126
Proverbs 4:1, 7, 8 - Levy, 418
Proverbs - Spies, 663
Prudentius, Clemens (348-410 A.D.) - Holst, 346
Prutz, R. - Bruckner, 131
Psalm 2:1-4 Wuorinen, 786
Psalm 4:1, 5:2 - Schütz, 634
Psalm 5 - Lassus, 414
Psalm 6 - Byrd, 141
Psalm 6 - Gill, 285
Psalm 8:1-2 - Marcello, 450
Psalm 10 - Marcello, 448
Psalm 13:16 - Marcello, 447
Psalm 14 - Marcello, 448
Psalm 17:5, 6 - Marcello, 449
Psalm 18 - Rogers, 589
Psalm 19:7-10 - Wyton, 791
Psalm 19:1-4 - Tomkins, 721
Psalm 22 - Marcello, 448
Psalm 23 - Leighton, 427
Psalm 23 - London, 434
Psalm 23 (paraphrased) - Pitfield, 561
Psalm 25 - Barrow, 49
Psalm 25 - Lassus, 414
Psalm 25 - Marcello, 448
Psalm 27:4 - Schütz, 633
Psalm 27:1-4 - Wuorinen, 786
Psalm 30 - Marcello, 448
Psalm 30 - Pisk, 556
Psalm 36:30, 31 - Binkerd, 93

Psalm 130 (paraphrased) - Purcell, 379
Psalm 133 - Sowerby, 662
Psalm 134 - Titcomb, 715
Psalm 134 - Tye, 725
Psalm 134 - Zimmerman, 795
Psalm 135:1 - Shepherd, 646
Psalm 137 - Ainsworth Psalter, 520
Psalm 137:1-4 - Mawby, 462
Psalm 140:2 - Binkerd, 95
Psalm 145 - Moe, 485
Psalm 148:1-9 - Bay Psalm Book, 520
Psalm 148:1-5 - Mawby, 462
Psalm 150 - Ainsworth Psalter, 520
Psalm 150 (Laudate eum) - Couture, 175
Psalm 150, 149, 145 - Davis, 202
Psalm 150 - Langlais, 409
Psalm 150 - Noss, 520

Quest, Clayton - Clockey, 164

Rabelais, François (1490-1553?) - Carter, 148
Reinick, Robert (1805-1852) - Henschel, 331
Reinick - Schumann, 630
Requiem Mass Text - Berlioz, 82
Requiem Mass Text - Cherubini, 157
Requiem Mass Text - Cornelius, 173
Requiem Mass Text - deSermisy, 216
Requiem Mass Text - Liszt, 425
Requiem Mass Text - Stravinsky, 682
Requiem Mass Text - Thomson, 714
Revelations 14:3 - Spohr, 664
Rhodes, W. - Beethoven, 59
Rice, Sir Cecil Spring (1859-1913) - Holst, 345
Rig Veda (from the Sacred Writings of Hinduism) - Holst, 343
Rilke, Rainer Maria (1875-1926) - Binkerd, 96
Roberts, Bill - Kubik, 398
Robinson, Edwin Meade (1878-?) - Wagner, 756
Roethke, Theodore - Kubik, 404
Romagnoli, Ettore (1871-1938) - Dalla Piccola, 195
Roman - Seraphic Missal - Binkerd, 89
Roman Breviary - Handl, 308
Romani, Felice (1788-1865) - Bellini, 62
Rossetti, Christina (1830-1894) - Binkerd, 98
Rosetti - Stevens, 672
Rossetti, Folgore da San Geminiano (fl1300-1332) - Ives, 357
Row, Richard - Sibelius, 650, 652, 654

Shakespeare, Twelfth Night (II, 3) - Washburn, 766
Shakespeare, Twelfth Night (II, 4) - Washburn, 766
Shakespeare, Much Ado About Nothing (II, 3) - Washburn, 766
Shao Ch'ang (Ch'ing Dynasty) - Korte, 389
Shelley, Percy (1792-1822) - Clarke, 160
Sheridan, Richard (1751-1816) - Kay, 369
Sh'vet Upanished 11, 17 - Hovhaness, 352
Silberstein, August - Bruckner, 127
Silesius, Angelus - Bacon, 38
Skelton, John (1460-1529) - Vaughan Williams, 728
Slovak, Folk - Bartók, 50
Smith, Elizabeth - Beeson, 56
Smith, Margery - Keenan, 371
Snyder, G. - Lora, 435
Social Harp (publ. 1868) - Frackenpohl, 270
Solomon 1:3, 2 - Handl, 311
Solomon 7:6, 7, 5, 4, 11, 12 - Henry VIII, 330
Sophocles (496?-406 B.C.) - Mendelssohn, 471
Sophocles - Stravinsky, 683
Songs of Innocence, Blake - Forest, 266
Spanenburg, Johann - Schütz, 635
Spender, Stephen (1909-) - Barber, 45
Stein, Gertrude (1874-1946) - Thomson, 711
Stephens, Peter John - Schubert, 615
Sterbini, Cesare - Rossini, 596
Sterne, Kenneth - Casals, 149
Stevens - Marcello, 449, 450, 477
Stevenson, Robert Louis (1850-1894) - Vaughan Williams, 734
Still, John (1543-1608) - Donovan, 233
Still - Vaughan Williams, 727
Strettel, Alma - Elgar, 248
Student Songs, 13th Cent. - Orff, 524, 525
Student Songs, University of Leipzig - Schein, 603
Suckling, Sir John (1609-1642) - Mills, 482, 483
Swenson - Luening, 442
Symonds, Arthur (1865-1945) - Delius, 213
Symonds - Kohn, 388

Taggard, Genevieve (1894-1948) - Schumann, 622
Tagore, Rabindranath (1861-1941) - Creston, 184, 188
Tagore - Korte, 392
Talmud - Bacon, 38
Tate, Alan (1899-) - Carter, 146
Taylor, Helen - Bantock, 42
Timothy 5:23 - Zelter, 794

INDEX OF FIRST LINES AND TITLES

176 Music for Men's Voices

Handful of Delights: Greensleeves - Vaughan Williams,
    729
Hear, Ye Children - Levy, 418
Heavens Declare the Glory of God, The - Tomkins, 721
Helgoland - Bruckner, 127
Here Is the God from Amour, tu as été - Crawford, 182
Here Is Thy Footstool - Creston, 184
Herod from A Boy Was Born - Britten, 116
Herodiade: Choeur des Romains - Massenet, 465
High Priests and Scribes from the Christmas Story - Schütz,
    637
Hoc signum crucis - Asola, 17
Hodie aparuit (On this Day) - Lassus, 413
Hodie, Christus natus est - Monteverdi, 492
Hodie, Christus natus est - Nanino, 510
Holiday Cruise - Clokey, 163
Holiday Song - Schuman, 622
Holy God We Praise Thy Name (Laudamus Te) - Mueller,
    509
Holy Spirit, Mass of The - Rorem, 592
Homesick Blues - Donato, 229
Hop Up, My Ladies - Kubik, 400
Hope for Tomorrow - Berger, 70
Hostias from Requiem Mass - Berlioz, 82
House Among the Trees, The - Ballantine, 39
How Merrily We Live - Este, 256
How Mighty are the Sabbaths - Holst, 346
Humble Shepherds, The - Davis, 203
Hunter's Farewell, The (Der Jäger Abschied) - Mendelssohn,
    473
Hush, Come Quickly from Rigoletto - Verdi, 743
Hush, My Dear - Barrow, 48
Hymn of Nativity - Serly, 643
Hymn to Agni, Soma, Manas, Indra - Holst, 343
Hymn to the Night - Word, 785
Hymne - Schubert, 613
Hymns to Eros - Strube, 684

I Am Black (Nigra sum) - Casals, 149
I Bought Me a Cat - Copland, 167
I Feel Death - Rorem, 591
I Give You a New Commandment - Shepherd, 647
I Go Before My Charmer - Morley, 498
I Have Lost All, from Amour tu as été - Crawford, 182
I Vow Thee My Country - Holst, 345
I Will Extol Thee - Moe, 485
I Will Lift Mine Eyes from Two Songs of Hope - Adler, 2

Mass in the Eighth Mode (Missa Octavi Toni) - Asola, 18
Mass in Three Parts (Missa Sine Nomine) - Byrd, 142
Mass in Unison or Two Parts - Becker, 54
Mass of the Good Shepherd - Pinkham, 553
Mass of the Holy Spirit - Rorem, 592
Mass, Repleatur os meum laude: Benedictus - Palestrina, 533
Mass to Honor St. John the Divine - Wyton, 790
Mass Without a Name (Missa Sine Nomine) - Asola, 18
Mater patris et filia - Brumel, 132
May the Sun Bless Us - Korte, 392
May God Abide from Two Anthems - Cruft, 192
Media Vita - Bruch, 120
Media Vita - Holler, 342
Meditation on the Syllable OM - Nelson, 513
Men of Harlech - Riegger, 587
Messe à Trois Voix - Caplet, 145
Messe cum Jubilo - Duruflé, 242
Messe de Notre Dame - Machaut, 445
Metsamiehen Laulu - Sibelius, 650
Miami L'Asaph - Pinkam, 554
Midnight Epilogue from Osolanda - Bantock, 40
Military Mass - Martinů, 454
Mille grazie from The Barber of Seville - Rossini, 596
Miniatures - Pitfield, 560
Miserere from Il Trovatore - Verdi, 739
Missa Adoro Te - Creston, 185
Missa Ave Maria - Morales, 497
Missa Brevis - Willan, 776
Missa Brevis à Troix Voix - Caplet, 145
Missa Brevis: Benedictus - Palestrina, 532
Missa Dona Nobis Pacem - Langlais, 407
Missa Duodecim Tonorum - Krenek, 397
Missa Fiat Voluntas Tuas - Andriessen, 7
Missa in Honorem Reginae Pacis - Peeters, 538
Missa in Honorem Sancti Lutgardis - Peeters, 539
Missa in Nativitatae - Pitoni, 562
Missa L'Homme Armé: Agnus Dei - Morales, 496
Missa Mater Patris - Des Prez, 217
Missa Octavi Toni (Mass in the Eighth Mode) - Asola, 18
Missa Pange Lingua: Pleni sunt caeli - Des Prez, 219
Missa pro Defunctis - Thomson, 714
Missa Quodlibetica - Luython, 443
Missa Salve Regina - Langlais, 408
Missa Sancti Joannis Evangelistae - Titcomb, 717
Missa Sanctus Ludovicus - Andriessen, 8
Missa Sine Nomine (Mass Without a Name) - Asola, 19

194   Music for Men's Voices

Psalm 133 - Sowerby, 662
Psalm 134 - Zimmerman, 795
Psalm 150: Laudate eum - Couture, 175
Psalm 150 - Langlais, 409
Psalm 150 - Newbury, 514
Psalms X, XII, XIV, XXV, XXX, XLII from Estro-Poetico-
 Armonico - Marcello, 448
Punch - Arne, 14

Quam pulchra es - Henry VII, 330
Quatre Prières de Saint François de Assise - Poulenc, 571
Queen of Spades: Now if Pretty Girls - Tchaikovsky, 701
Quem iridistis pastores - Deering, 207
Quid sum miser from Requiem Mass - Berlioz, 82
Quis multa gracilis from Six Odes of Horace - Thompson,
 703

Recognition of the Land (Landerkennung) - Grieg, 298
Regina Caeli (O Be Joyful) - Aichinger, 4
Regum mundi from Opus Musicum Harmoniarum - Handl,
 308
Rejoice in the Lord - Causton, 150
Remember Me - Stevens, 672
Repleti sunt omnes - Handl, 309
Requiem - Berlioz, 83
Requiem aeternam (Calm Repose Eternal) - Cornelius, 173
Requiem in D Minor - Cherubini, 157
Requiem Mass for Male Voices - Liszt, 425
Reveille, The - Elgar, 249
Resonet in laudibus (Let the Voice of Praise Resound) -
 Handl, 310
Revelation of St. John the Divine - Argento, 13
Rhapsodie Hassidique - Kahn, 366
Rienzi: Battle Hymn - Wagner, 763
Rig Veda, Hymns from the - Holst, 343
Righteous Living Forever, The (Periti autem) - Mendelssohn,
 476
Rigoletto: Zitti, Zitti - Verdi, 743
Rinaldo - Brahms, 110
Ritornelle - Schumann, 629
Romeo and Juliet: Serenade of the Capulets - Berlioz, 83
Round, Around About a Wood - Morley, 499
Rose Stood in the Dew, The - Schumann, 625
Ruins, The - Kodály, 381
Rustics and Fisherman from Gloriana - Britten, 114

Sacrae Cantiunculae - Monteverdi, 493

200   Music for Men's Voices

Vagabond, The - Vaughan Williams, 734
Vagabond King, The: Song of the Vagabonds - Friml, 276
Vale of Tuoni - Sibelius, 645
V'al Y'de Avodecho - Lewandowski, 420
Variation über ein altes Tanzlied - Hindemith, 339
Venezuela - Niles, 518
Veni, sponsa Christi (Come Thou Faithful Servant) - Monte-
    verdi, 494
Verba mea auribus from Three Psalms - Lassus, 414
Verbum caro factum est (God Now Dwells Among Us) - Has-
    sler, 323
Vere languores nostros (Surely He Hath Borne Our Griefs)
    - Lotti, 439
Verleeh uns frieden - Hammerschmidt, 305
Vier Männerstimme - Busoni, 138
Villanelle - Massenet, 458
Vision des Mannes from Drei Männerchöre - Hindemith,
    340
Vision of Belshazzar - Bantock, 43
Viva Augusta from Ernani - Verdi, 736
Vom Frühjahr - Orff, 528
Vom Rhein - Bruch, 118

Wanderer's Song - Delius, 213
Was betrübst du dich - Schubert, 636
Was gleicht auf Erden from Der Freischütz - Weber, 768
Water Parted from the Sea - Arne, 15
Weep O Mine Eyes - Wilbye, 775
Welcome Yule - Willan, 779
We Sail the Ocean Blue - Sullivan, 687
We Suffer Sore, by Sin (Cantata 136) - Bach, 29
Whether I Find Thee from Five Part Songs - Elgar, 248
While Steadfastly They Watched (Cantata 11) - Bach, 23
Who Shall Speak for the People - Kurka, 405
Why Afflict They Self - Schütz, 636
Why so Pale and Wan - Mills, 483
Widerspruch (Contradiction) - Schubert, 618
William Tell: Coro di cacciatori e di svizzeri - Rossini,
    595
William Tell: Song of the Monks - Beethoven, 61
Wine of the Grape - Korte, 393
Wir Lieben sehr (With Our Hearts) - Friderici, 275
Wisdom Exalteth Her Children - Nowak, 521
Wise Men from the East from The Christmas Story - Schütz,
    638
With Cat Like Tread from Pirates of Penzance - Sullivan,
    688